HOME
MAKERS'
GUIDE

ALLIANCE ✚ LEICESTER

STAFF CREDITS

Editor Mary Devine

Art Editor Helen James

Consultant Mike Lawrence

Production Craig Chubb

Special Sales Will Steeds

A MARSHALL CAVENDISH BOOK

© Marshall Cavendish Limited 1990

First printing 1990
Reprinted 1991
3 4 5 6 7 8 9   99 98 97 96 95 94 93 92 91

**Concept, design and production by
Marshall Cavendish Books (Special Sales)
58 Old Compton Street, London W1V 5PA**

Typesetting by Litho Link Ltd, Welshpool, Powys, Wales
Printed in Portugal

ISBN 1-85435-326-8

PICTURE CREDITS

FRONT COVER PHOTO COURTESY OF **ALLIED MAPLES**

7 Harry Clow; 8, 9 btm, 10, 11, 12 Gareth Trevor; 9 top
Kevin Jones; 13, 15, 16, 17 Alan Marsh; 14 Kevin Jones;
19, 20 Paul Emra; 24-5 Harry Clow; 28-9 btm Peter Reilly.
28-9 top Rentokil; 26 Spectrum Colour Library; 28 Chris
Taylor; 30 ROSPA; 32-3 top Building Research Establish-
ment; 32 btm Chubb Fire Security Ltd; 46 Crown Wallcoverings; 47 btm Paul Emra; 47 top, 48-50 Alan Marsh;
40, 44 mid left ICI Paints Division; 42 btm right, 43 btm, 45
btm Barnaby's Picture Library; 41 Kevin Jones; 42 top mid
+ btm left Crown Paints; 43 top right Nitromors; 45 top
Mosley-Stone Ltd; 51 top H & R Johnson Tiles Ltd; 52 top
left + btm; 53, 54 btm mid + btm right Steve Lyne; 52 left
+ top right, 54 top + btm left Paul Emra; 56-7 btm, 58 top
Kuo Kan Chen; 56-7 top, 58 btm, 60 Alan Marsh; 59 Steve
Lyne; 61 Rentokil; 65-8 Alan Marsh; 66 Paul Emra

CONTENTS

FOREWORD

Dear Homemaker

Welcome to your new home and thank you for arranging your mortgage through Alliance & Leicester.

You will, of course, wish to look after and improve your home. The Alliance & Leicester HomeMakers' Guide is just the book you need since it contains up-to-date information on a wide range of home-related topics.

With thanks to Laura Ashley

If ever you require information or advice on any aspect of your mortgage, then please do contact your local Alliance & Leicester branch. Our branch staff can also help you with your insurance and investment questions as well as Home Improvement and Personal Loans.

In the meantime, happy homemaking.

Customer Services

Security is required for Home Improvement Loans and some Personal Loans.
Written quotations are available on request.

YOUR HOME IS AT RISK IF YOU DO NOT KEEP UP REPAYMENTS ON A MORTGAGE OR OTHER LOAN SECURED ON IT.

HOME SECURITY

How burglar-proof is your home? No-one can afford to be complacent, so check out your home security now.

Being burgled is an unpleasant experience for several reasons. It is not just a question of losing possessions, although that can be hurtful enough if the items stolen had sentimental value or were unique. There is also the damage done to property: broken furniture, smashed ornaments, even graffiti-covered walls. And then there are feelings of vulnerability, nervousness and fear that it will happen again. Luckily, you can reduce your chances of it ever happening by becoming security conscious. But it is advisable to make certain that you are fully insured, just in case.

Most burglaries are carried out by opportunists taking advantage of people's 'it could never happen to me' attitude and of their carelessness. It is neither difficult nor expensive to protect your home against this type of burglar: even the most basic security measures have a deterrent effect. Rather than risk unwanted attention by loitering in a porch or smashing glass, the average burglar will give up, move on or have a go elsewhere.

How do burglars get in?
Burglars always choose the easy way in, usually through an unlocked door or open window. So the first rule of home security is to close and lock – always. Never leave a window unfastened or door on the latch because you are 'only popping round to the neighbour's for five minutes'. In less time than that, a dishonest passer-by can sneak in and remove portable items like your jewellery, video or credit cards.

When you are at home, it is always best to keep the front door locked, but especially if you are busy upstairs or in the garden. Similarly, ground-floor windows facing the street should be closed securely if you are not actually in the room concerned.

After dark
When you go out in the evening, discourage intruders by leaving a light on in a downstairs room – but not the hall, experienced burglars are all too familiar with this particular 'ruse'. Remember to close the curtains, too, and leaving a radio on will add to the impression that someone is at home. If you are frequently out after dark, fit an automatic time switch which will turn the lights on at dusk and then switch them on and off at random intervals throughout the evening. It is also helpful to leave a light on in the front porch: a burglar intent on forcing a lock wants to be inconspicuous.

Burglar alarms
Basic security measures, like locks and bolts, will deter opportunist burglars, but not professional thieves. So, if you have valuable possessions in your home you should consider installing a burglar alarm (*see* **Burglar Alarms**). There are various alarm systems on the market, some suitable for DIY fitting, others requiring expert installation. Before choosing a system, seek advice: the police and insurance companies will be happy to advise you.

Outside security
Strong locks on garages and sheds are essential to prevent garden implements and DIY tools from being stolen or used to force an entry into the house. Choose padlocks with a hoop (shackle) that sits tight against the body lock because these are more difficult to force. As a further precaution fit a heavy-duty padlock bar with concealed fixing screws.

Ladders give instant access to upstairs windows, so never leave a ladder lying about in the garden or in an unlocked garden shed or garage. If the ladder is too long to store in a garage or shed, chain its sections together and padlock it to a solid fixture like a drainpipe, tree or stout fence post.

Any gate between the front of the house and the back should also have a secure lock, and all fences should be kept in good repair.

Protecting your car
Car security is quite straightforward – just follow this checklist:

● Do not keep the insurance certificate, registration document and other important papers in the car.
● Hide any belongings which might tempt a thief – preferably in a locked boot.
● Do not leave property on the seats, back shelf or roof rack.
● If your car has a steering-column lock, use it every time; if it doesn't have one use an immobiliser.
● Fasten all windows, including quarter lights and sun roof.
● Lock all doors, boot or tailgate.
● Always remove the ignition keys when the car is not in use, even when garaged. Also, remember to park your car in a well-lit place at night: thieves like shadows.
● Never leave children or animals alone in a parked car: with a window open you risk theft; with the windows closed, suffocation.

The following chapter offers further security advice together with practical projects that will help you to protect your home and valuables.

THINK SECURITY

The casual thief isn't looking for a wealthy household, he is looking for an empty house with an easy way in – like an unlatched downstairs window. If there are valuables on show, and no witnesses around, so much the better for the burglar.

To deter the thief, always secure doors and windows before you go out – don't leave even the smallest window open for pets. Never leave expensive portable items such as a video recorder or camera clearly visible from the street because these are an instant temptation – particularly if the window is unfastened. Keep them out of sight or hang sheer curtains across front windows.

Always remember to shut the garage doors when you go out: a wide-open empty garage is a sure sign that nobody is at home. Alert neighbours are a great asset, and neighbourhood watch schemes have proved very effective.

Front-door security
As a standard fitting, most front doors have a rim lock with cylinder nightlatch, which automatically locks when the door is pulled shut. But nightlatches can easily be opened with a piece of plastic like a credit card. For maximum security, therefore, fit a mortise deadlock (see **Secure Your Front Door**) as well. This

Secure locks on front and back windows, as well as windows that can be reached from a flat roof, will deter the opportunist burglar.

type of lock can only be operated with a key and, because it is set into the door itself, forcing it is very difficult. Whatever type of lock you install, it will only be as strong as the surrounding wood, so check that your frame and door are sound before fitting. Then, be careful with the key; do not leave it inside the letter flap or in the inside lock (it can be turned from the outside).

There are several other security measures suitable for front doors: strong bolts fitted at top and bottom; a chain which prevents the door being opened more than a crack – allowing safe scrutiny of unexpected visitors, and a peephole or spyhole set into the door at eye-level height, which gives a wide-angle view of the doorstep so that you can see and identify callers without opening the door at all.

Check before opening
If an unknown visitor claims to be an official, such as a policeman, gas inspector or telephone engineer, do not let him in – even if he is wearing uniform – without first asking to see his identity card. If you still have doubts, make him wait outside while you phone the head office. He will probably leave quickly at this point if he is not genuine, but if you want to be extra cautious, do not accept the telephone number that you are given by the caller. Instead, telephone the operator to check the number. Genuine visitors will understand your reasons for taking extra security precautions and will not mind waiting.

Back-door security
Back doors, and all other external doors, should also be fitted with a strong mortise lock. In addition, fit a bolt at the top and bottom of the door. A conventional, surface-mounted bolt is better than nothing, but it can be pulled back (through a broken, glazed panel) and it will only resist a certain amount of pressure. A better option is to fit mortise rack bolts which are set into the edge of the door and then operated by a key.

French doors
French doors usually have a mortise lock, but for extra security fit bolts vertically – perferably mortise rack – to the top and bottom of both doors. If the doors open outwards, guard against removal (by lifting of the hinges) by fitting hinge bolts at the top and bottom of each door.

Make your windows secure
For burglars, windows are a popular point of entry. So always shut and secure all windows when you go out, including those upstairs as thieves can, and do, climb drainpipes. Skylights and windows near flat roofs are almost as vulnerable as those on the ground floor; so all these windows should be fitted with proper locks.

Watch Points

Going Out?
Make sure that you have:
● **Locked all doors and windows**
● **Set the burglar alarm**
● **At night, leave a light on – but not just in the hall or porch**

Where to keep valuables:
● **Not in the house, if possible**
● **Not on view**
● **Keep small valuables in a safe deposit or install your own safe**
● **Identify valuable goods with your own marks and keep full, written details of them (special pens for marking all sorts of surfaces and materials are now available at many hardware shops).**

A wide range of locks is available to suit the various types of window: casement, sash, skylight, wood frame and metal. Most models are operated by key, and some even allow the window to remain slightly open for ventilation when locked. To choose the most appropriate lock for your needs, take a sketch of your window and frame, together with dimensions, to a security centre.

Certain windows have special problems. Louvred windows, for example, easily lift out of their frame. One solution is to stick each piece of glass into the frame with epoxy resin glue. A more extreme measure is to fit a grille or bars across the window; some grilles open and close like curtains. Window-mounted extractor fans can also be removed quite easily. If you are installing one, position it in a fixed window or well out of reach of fastenings. Alternatively, fit key-operated window locks and keep the key hidden.

Moving home – safely
When you move into a new home, check out its security thoroughly, paying special attention to locks. If the mortised locks have registered keys (this is a service operated by some manufacturers whereby keys are only issued against the registered owner's signature) make sure you have all the keys that have been issued. If one is missing – or if the keys are not registered – then you should change the lock.

Home safes — worthwhile or not?
If, for some unavoidable reason, you have to keep large sums of cash in the house or you possess pieces of precious jewellery, you might consider installing a home safe.

There are two types available for home use: floor safes, sited under the floorboards where they are embedded in concrete, and wall safes, set into the wall and hidden by a mirror or picture.

The smallest models are the size of a standard brick; the largest are about five bricks high. Some models have a keylock, others a combination lock with thousands of permutations.

Keep outhouses, sheds and garages securely locked – use a sturdy padlock. Make sure, too, that ladders are not left lying about.

Holiday-Time Do's and Don'ts

There are several steps you can take to reduce the risk of break-ins while you are on holiday:

● DO NOT tell everyone you meet that you are going away.
● DO tell a trusted neighbour and, if you are away for a long time, also tell the police.
● DO make sure that you cancel daily deliveries like milk and newspapers.
● DO trim your front lawn in summer before going away. An unkempt lawn in front of an otherwise tidy house signals to a burglar that the house is empty.
● DO try to arrange for a neighbour to go into your home from time to time to remove mail jammed in the letterflap (especially important if you receive free newspapers and circulars every week). Similarly, piled up mail or newspapers on the doormat must be moved if the front door is glazed.
● DO ask your neighbour to switch lights on and off in your home occasionally. Alternatively, fit timer-operated light switches that automatically turn on and off at pre-set times after dark so that the house appears to be occupied.
● DO NOT close the curtains: this looks odd during the day and will makes thieves curious.
● DO NOT lock inside doors: once burglars have broken in, locked doors will not stop them and will only result in more damage.
● DO fasten all windows securely, lock and bolt the back door and then lock the front door behind you. Take the key with you!

SECURE YOUR FRONT DOOR

Burglary seems to be a growth industry these days, especially in urban areas. Not surprisingly, home owners are fighting back and taking steps to protect their homes by fitting an increasingly sophisticated array of home security devices. The area that needs the most thorough protection of all is your front door.

It's comparatively easy to secure doors and windows from the inside by fitting bolts and locks. The most difficult job is securing the door you use to make your final exit from the house – usually your front door – because you have to lock it from the outside. This means fitting a lock (or locks: many people now fit two) that is securely attached to the door without weakening its construction, cannot be prised, cut or drilled open and is proof against picking or the use of skeleton keys. There is a wide range of suitable locks available, and fitting them is a comparatively straightforward do-it-yourself job. Alternatively, you can employ a locksmith or carpenter to do the job for you.

The other weak spots in any door are the hinges; a burglar may attempt to force the door open at this side with a crowbar inserted between door and frame. You can reinforce the hinge side of your front door by adding small steel hinge bolts that fit into recesses in the door frame when the door is closed.

You may also want to improve your door's security when you're in. If you have a solid door, a door viewer allows you to check the identity of callers before admitting them, while a door chain or bar prevents an intruder from bursting into the house as you open the door. Both these devices are quick and simple to install.

What the job involves

Making your front door secure is simply a matter of buying the right products and fitting them to your existing door, either as replacements for what is there already or as additional security. The job involves the following steps:
● Check your existing front door locks (see **Curing faults**)

● Decide what type of lock – mortise or rim lock – you want to fit
● Choose a model that will fit your door (you need to measure the lock stile's width and thickness) and is marked as conforming to British Standard BS3621 (it may also carry the BS Kite mark)
● Fit the lock to your door, following the manufacturer's instructions carefully
● Add other security accessories such as hinge bolts, a door viewer and a door chain or bar.

BEFORE YOU START . . .
● Check the condition of your existing lock (see **Curing faults**) so you can decide whether you need a brand new replacement or just some additional security devices.
● Decide on whether you want a mortise or a rim lock. Mortise locks have the advantage that they are almost inaccessible to a would-be burglar, but fitting one can weaken the door structure. Cylinder locks are easier to fit, but may also be easier to force unless they are carefully installed. Fitting one of each may be a good solution, especially if you rely at present on just a rim lock.

● Measure the width and thickness of the door stile – the vertical part of the door to which the lock will be fitted. Most exterior doors are at least 38mm (1½in) thick, but some mortise locks require a door thickness of as much as 48mm(1⅞in). Both types generally need a stile about 85mm(3⅜in) wide, though models are available for use on glazed and panel doors with narrow stiles.

Checklist

Tools and materials
tape measure and pencil
mortise gauge (mortise locks only)
brace and auger bits *or*
    electric drill and flat wood bits
chisels and mallet
screwdrivers
junior hacksaw (rim locks only)
bradawl
padsaw
lock and staple to BS3621
two hinge bolts
door viewer
door chain/bar

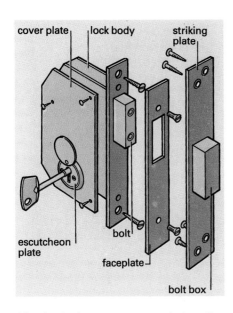

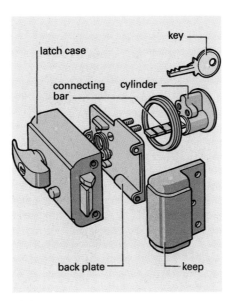

Mortise locks are strong and virtually burglar-proof, but could weaken your door structure

Cylinder locks must be installed carefully, especially if they are to be the only lock on your front door

worn cylinder is a keyhole position slightly off the vertical.

● If you have an automatic deadlock type, check that the smaller secondary bolt does not enter the staple (it should be pressed in by contact with the face of the striking plate as the door is closed). If it does, the deadlock won't work. Now press the smaller bolt in and check that it has locked the main bolt so it cannot be pushed in. Check that the double-locking action actually locks the inside knob.

● If any lock needs a lot of fiddling to get it to work, take it to a locksmith for an overhaul (remember to leave someone in the house while the lock is off!). Never oil a stiff lock; use powdered graphite (from locksmiths).

Use powdered graphite to lubricate a stiff lock – pour on to the key and work into the lock

● Choose a style and finish that suits your door. Rim locks come in a range of metallic and coloured finishes. The visible parts of mortise locks are usually brass or bright steel, but you can buy handles (for locks incorporating a latch mechanism as well) and keyhole (escutcheon) plates in a wide range of attractive finishes.

WATCH OUT FOR . . .

● Weak or rotten doors and frames. It's no good fitting a top of the range lock in a weak door or a rotten door frame. If yours are definitely past their prime, it may be worth installing a new, stronger door (and frame) first.

● Narrow stiles (see above). If you have stiles less than about 75mm(3in) wide, you will have to fit a lock specially designed for narrow stiles.

● Key security. You usually get two or three keys with the lock, and in most cases you can get extra keys cut by a locksmith or a local key-cutting service. Some manufacturers offer a key registration service, which means your name is recorded and you can get extra keys only from them, against your authorized signature.

● Deadlockability. This means that the bolt of the lock cannot be pushed back once the door is shut, and can be opened only with a key. Some cheap

cylinder rim nightlatches cannot be deadlocked, and should not be used on exterior doors. Some rim locks have a spring bolt that deadlocks automatically when the door is closed; other locks of this type must be deadlocked by an extra turn of the key.

● Double-throw locks. These have a special mechanism that throws the bolt further into the staple if the key is given a second turn. If you turn the key only once, it may not project as far as a single-throw bolt would, and so may be marginally less secure.

Curing faults

Before you consider replacing an existing lock, check its action and performance carefully.

● Close and lock the door. If this is hard to do, check whether the door has dropped on its hinges; the bolt may be binding on the top or bottom of the staple, and forcing the lock may have worn the key. Scrap a worn lock.

● Turn the lock with the door open and try to push the bolt back in. If you can, replace the lock.

● With a cylinder lock, try to withdraw the key before it is in the locked position. If you can, change the cylinder or scrap the lock. Another sign of a

Fitting a mortise lock

The only tricky thing about fitting a mortise lock is cutting a neat mortise in the door edge. Power tools can help if you think you're not a dab hand with chisel and mallet.

Start by selecting the position for the lock. If it will be the only lock on the door, position it at about waist height; if you are planning on having a rim lock as well, fit it a bit lower – say one-third of the way up the door – for maximum security. The rim lock will go about two-thirds of the way up.

Unpack the lock and read the instructions carefully so you can identify all the components and, most importantly, you know which fixing screw goes where.

Wedge the door open before you start working on it. Alternatively, remove it from its hinges so you can work on a horizontal edge – perhaps held in a Workmate. If you do this, work on it where you can keep an eye on the unguarded door opening.

Mark the position and height of the mortise on the door edge using the lock body as a template. Then set a mortise gauge to match the thickness of the lock body, and mark the width of the mortise.

The quickest way of cutting the mortise is to use a power drill and a wood bit the same diameter as the lock body. Drill the holes slightly too deep so that any debris left in the mortise will be unable to foul the lock body when it is inserted.

The drilled holes must be at right angles to the door edge. Use a drill guide if you have one to ensure this; otherwise sight the drill against a try square held against the door edge.

Pare down the edges of the drilled-out mortise with a chisel and test the fit of the lock body. When you are sure that it will slide in fully, mark round the fore-end of the lock so you can cut the shallow recess in the door edge to accept it. Remove the lock and cut round the edges of this recess before paring away the waste wood carefully.

Test the fit of the lock body again. Then remove it, hold it against the face of the door with its fore-end flush with the door edge and use a bradawl to mark the position of the keyhole. Drill the hole right through the door (hold some scrap wood against the other side to stop the wood splintering as the drill emerges) and use a padsaw to cut the sides of the keyhole slot. Finally use a narrow chisel to cut out the waste, and a fine wood file to clean up the slot.

Insert the lock body into its mortise for the last time, and check that the key fits easily into the lock and operates it smoothly. Then drive in the fixing screws that secure the lock to the door edge, and add the escutcheon plates to each face of the door.

Chalk the end of the lock bolt. Close the door and operate the lock to mark

where it touches the door frame. Use this mark as a guide for cutting out the mortise and shallow recess into which the metal staple will be fixed. Test its fit, and check that the lock bolt enters it centrally without fouling the sides, top or bottom before you screw it into place.

If you are worried that your door has been over-weakened by the cutting of the mortise, fit metal strengthening plates containing keyholes to each face of the door. They should extend for at least 150mm(6in) above and below the mortise position, and for security the exterior plate should be fixed with clutch-head screws (or cross-slot screws with the recesses deformed).

1 Once the position of the lock has been marked, use a mortise gauge to mark the width of the mortise

2 Drill out the mortise, then pare edges with a chisel, removing all the debris for a good fit

3 Mark the keyhole position carefully with a bradawl, using the mortise lock as a template

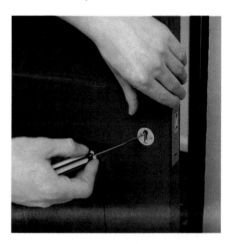

4 Once the keyholes have been cut, and the lock inserted, screw on the escutcheon plates

Fitting a rim lock

A securely-fixed deadlockable rim lock can be almost as secure as a mortise lock provided that the door is sound and the fixings are strong. If you fix one in addition to a mortise lock, you can have a door that is easy to open to admit visitors, and yet is doubly secure when you go out.

A cylinder rim lock is easier to fit than a mortise lock; all you have to do is drill a hole through the door big enough to take the cylinder, chisel out a shallow recess in the door frame to accept the staple and drive in a few screws.

As with a mortise lock, you need to start by unpacking the lock and very carefully identifying all the individual components contained in the pack.

TIP . . .

If the fixing screws supplied look a bit on the short side, there's no reason why you shouldn't substitute longer ones. The ones holding the lock backplate to the door can match the door thickness in length, while those driven through the staple at right angles to the frame should at least match the frame thickness and those driven at right angles to the door plane (i.e., parallel to the frame) can be even longer.

The first step is to decide on the lock position – just below shoulder height if it's the only lock on the door, two thirds of the way up the door if a mortise lock is also being fitted. Then use the lock backplate (or a template if one is supplied) to mark the cylinder position on the door's inner face, and drill a hole of the required size using a wood bit.

TIP . . .

If you haven't got a wood bit big enough, drill a series of small holes within the outline of the larger one, and cut out the waste with a narrow chisel (or even a coping saw). Clean up the hole with a half-round file.

Offer up the backplate again to the inner face of the door, and mark the positions for its fixing screws using a bradawl. Make pilot holes for the screws and drive them in to secure the backplate in position.

Next, slip the outer collar or door pull over the cylinder and insert the cylinder in its hole from the outer face of the door. Drive the machine screws supplied with the lock through the backplate into the lugs in the rear face of the cylinder to hold it securely in place.

Now use a junior hacksaw to cut off the connecting bar down to the required length to match the door thickness, and offer up the lock casing over the backplate with the end of the connecting bar engaged positively in the slot in the casing. With some models you engage the lock body over lugs in the faceplate and then slide it slightly towards the hinge edge of the door to lock it in position.

To complete the lock installation, drive in the small, stubby machine screws through the edge of the lock casing to secure it to the backplate.

Now close the door and mark the position of the staple on the door frame. Offer up the staple to mark out the recess for its striking plate, and chisel this out carefully to the required depth. Then drill pilot holes for the fixing screws, drive them in fully and check that the lock works smoothly. If the bolt catches on the edges of the staple, reposition it slightly.

TIP . . .

Check the tightness of all machine screws within a rim lock from time to time. Regular slamming of the door can cause them to work gradually loose.

Fitting hinge bolts

Hinge bolts are hardened steel pegs that are fitted into the hinged edge of the door and located in recesses drilled in the door frame. These prevent a would-be intruder from forcing the door from the outside.

Mark the bolt positions on the door edge, just below the hinge positions (fit three bolts if there are three hinges). Then fit a depth stop on your drill and drill holes of the required diameter into the door edge. Make sure you drill at right angles to the edge.

Hammer the ribbed end of the bolt

1 Mark the edge where the centre of the cylinder will go, then drill the hole in the door

2 Insert cylinder, then fix machine screws into the lugs at the rear face of the cylinder

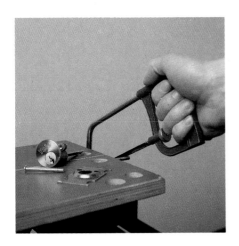

3 Cut the connecting bar and screws to the required length according to the depth of your door

4 Fit the lock casing over the backplate, engaging the connecting bar in the casing slot

into the hole, then partially close the door so the end of the bolt makes a mark on the frame. Measure the length of bolt protruding from the door, and drill a hole in the frame slightly deeper than this measurement. Again, use a depth stop when drilling.

Most hinge bolts come with a small keeper plate, which must be recessed into the door frame at each hole position. Offer the plate up, mark round it and chisel out the recess before screwing it into place. Make sure the countersunk screws are not proud of the plate surface, or they will foul the door edge when the door is closed. Check that the bolt enters the hole without touching the keeper as you close the door. You will need to reposition it slightly if it does.

Mark round the keeper plate, then chisel out the recess. Make sure the plate is flush with the frame

Fitting a door chain

A door chain or bar prevents a would-be intruder from barging in as you open the door. Its strength depends entirely on the strength of the fixings used.

Fixing a door chain or bar could not be easier. You attach the plate carrying the chain or bar to the edge of the door frame, and the keeper over which the chain or bar is hooked to the inner face of the door, close to the other plate.

Fix the door keeper first, marking the position of its fixing screws with a bradawl and drilling pilot holes in the wood. Use screws as long as the door thickness to get the best possible grip.

Then attach the plate to the door frame, again using long screws so they penetrate deep into the frame and cannot be torn out by attempted forced entry. If necessary, attach the bar or chain before driving the final fixing screw. Check that you can hook the chain or bar onto the keeper – and remove it – easily.

1 Mark the position of the fixing screws on the door frame with a bradawl, then drill pilot holes

2 Make sure the chain can be removed from the keeper and secured again easily

Fitting a door viewer

A door viewer is a useful accessory to fit if you have a solid door and no other means of identifying callers. Fit it centrally, at (or close to) eye level.

When you've marked the position of the viewer on the door, drill a hole of the

required diameter – usually about 12mm (½in) – through the door with a hand drill, brace and bit, or electric drill.

TIP . . .

If you're using an electric drill, get a helper to hold a piece of scrap wood against the outer face of the door while you drill the hole, to stop the wood from splintering when the drill tip bursts through to the other side.

Now push the barrel of the viewer into the hole from outside until the flange is flush with the door surface. Complete the job by screwing the eyepiece on to the inner end of the barrel using a coin or screwdriver.

1 Carefully insert the barrel of the door viewer into the hole from the outside of the door

2 Screw the eyepiece on to the barrel from the inside of the door, tighten with a screwdriver

LOCK YOUR WINDOWS

Windows are frequently neglected by homeowners when it comes to improving home security; they don't look particularly vulnerable, but they're a favourite means of entry to a house for many burglars.

A burglar will use a window to gain access to your home in one of three ways. If you leave it open, he'll simply climb in. If you shut it, he may break the glass, especially if it is a small-paned window, so he can reach in, operate the catch and open it. Or he may simply force the window with a crowbar or similar tool, hoping to wrench out the screws holding the catch to the frame. This last method highlights the weakness of any security product – it's only as strong as its fixing screws, and these are often woefully inadequate. Since many window locks are also screwed in place, look carefully at the screws supplied with window lock kits.

There are a great many window locks on the market. They fall into three broad groups. The first type stops the cockspur (the side catch on a casement window) from being operated; some replace it with a lockable version. The next category of locks secures the casement or fanlight stay in place. Products in both groups are surface-mounted. The last type of lock actually bolts the casement or fanlight to the frame, and may be surface-mounted or recessed. Most are designed for wood windows, but there are versions in each group for metal windows too. Your selection depends on what level of security you want, how much you're prepared to pay for it and what sort of finish you require.

What the job involves

As with doors, making your windows secure is a straightforward job – you just select the locks you need and fit them in position. You have to:
● Decide what type of lock you want to fit. In some cases this will depend not only on the window type and material but also on what sort of window catches or stays are already present
● Fit the lock to your window, following the manufacturer's instructions

● Put the key somewhere out of sight of would-be intruders, but visible from indoors so the window can be opened as a means of escape in case of fire.

BEFORE YOU START . . .
● Check that the casement or fanlight you want to lock is a close fit within the frame rebate. If not, the locks may not be very effective or may not work at all.
● See whether you can get locks in a finish that matches the rest of your window fittings. Many have white or silver finishes, but some are also available in brass. It's also worth noting how obtrusive the lock will be when seen from outside.
● Look at the locking action. The best type – in the sense that you can't fail to use it – is the snap-lock, which locks automatically as the window is closed. Types you have to screw in and out are more time-consuming to operate, and are less likely to be used all the time.
● Check whether key-operated types have key differs – each lock needing a different key. These are more secure than those operated by a universal key.
● Think about ventilation. Some stay-locks allow the casement or fanlight to be locked in a slightly open position –

useful for stopping children from falling out, but not to be relied on when the house is empty because they're easily forced from outside.
● Identify any casements or fanlights which are seldom, if ever, opened. It's not worth buying locks for these; instead, simply drive screws through the side of the opening part into the frame to secure them. Remember, though, that such windows cannot readily be used as fire escapes.

WATCH OUT FOR . . .
● Weak or rotten woodwork. It's no good fitting a lock that could be forced due to inadequate fixings.

Checklist

Tools and materials
pencil
try square
bradawl
electric drill and bits
chisels and mallet (recessed types)
screwdrivers
metal primer (metal windows only)

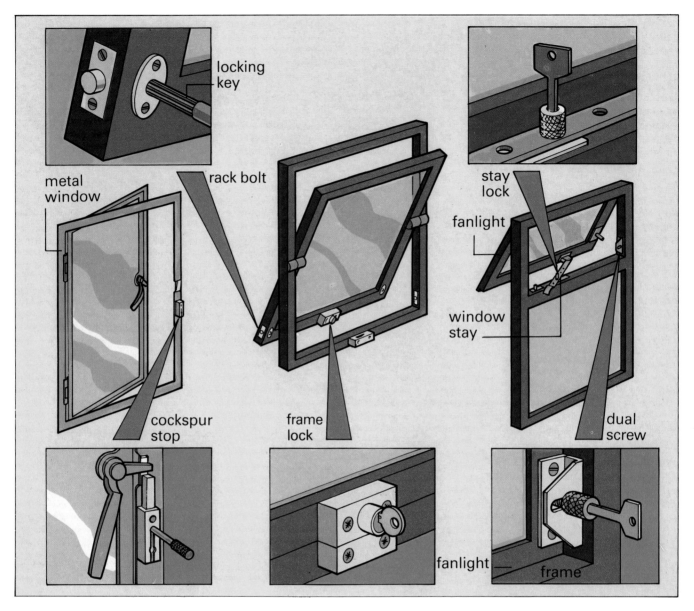

locking
key

metal
window

rack bolt

stay
lock

fanlight

window
stay

cockspur
stop

frame
lock

dual
screw

fanlight

frame

Window locks – in various types and finishes – hold opening part of wood or metal window to frame

● Inadequate fixing screws. If the screws supplied with the lock are visibly inadequate – too short, or too small a gauge – don't be afraid to substitute bigger ones.

● Narrow frames. If you have frames less than about 38mm(1½in) thick, recessed locks could weaken the woodwork unacceptably.

● Windows containing sealed-unit double glazing, especially those with aluminium frames. Take care not to damage the glazing units when you drill the fixing holes.

● Rust traps on steel windows. Any holes you drill should be treated with primer or a rust inhibitor before fixings are made.

● Plastic-framed windows. It is very difficult to fit conventional window locks to this type of window, and specialist advice should be sought – either from the window manufacturer, or, in the UK, from the British Plastics Federation (*see* **Datafile**: Windows).

Fitting a cockspur stop

A cockspur stop is attached to the window frame and prevents the handle from being lifted. Alternatively, the existing cockspur fastener can be replaced by a lockable one.

Cockspur stops are most commonly used on metal windows, and are surface-mounted (with some sliding-wedge types, the stop may fit within the channelling of the window frame). The body of the stop may contain a sliding bolt that moves up to locate against the catch part of the fastener, or may itself slide or swivel into and out of place. Most are unobtrusive from inside and noticeable from outside. Some are locked by a push-button action, others with a key (with or without differs). If the original cockspur has two catch positions, these can still be used to provide a minimum of ventilation in a room, with the stop in operation.

Fitting is extremely simple, although details may vary from manufacturer to manufacturer. Start by closing the window fully. Then offer up the lock body in the locked position and mark the position of the fixing screws on the window frame. Check that they will not interfere with the edge of the glass or double glazing. Then drill out the holes, using the drill size specified by the lock manufacturer. Open the window first to stop the bit damaging the casement once it has gone through the frame.

TIP . . .

To stop the drill bit from skidding as you start to drill the fixing holes, mark their positions with a centrepunch first and locate the drill tip in the depression before switching on.

Now simply attach the lock body and any gaskets using the self-tapping screws provided and check that the fastener operates smoothly.

Locking cockspur fasteners are intended to replace the existing fastener on wooden windows; they're not suitable for metal windows. Some brands are handed left or right, so make sure that you get the correct one to suit your window.

To fit one, start by removing the old latch and catch, then carefully fill the old fixing holes and prime any bare wood that's exposed.

Next, get a helper to hold the casement closed while you attach the new fastener to it. You can then position the catch in relation to it, and screw it to the frame. Lock the latch in the closed position and check that it is secure.

5. *The alternative type of stop clamps on to cockspur. Lock by tightening screw with key provided*

TIP . . .

For added security, attach the components with cross-head screws and drill out the cross so the screws cannot be undone even if they can be reached through a broken window pane.

Fitting a stay lock

Stay locks can be used to secure the stay of any window and prevent it being lifted off its pin or keeper.

There are three types of casement stay available. Type 1 is used instead of (or in addition to) the pin on the frame over which the holes in the stay are located. Type 2 is used with solid stays – the kind with locating recesses on the underside, but no holes. Both are for wooden windows; only the first can provide ventilation. Type 3 is designed for metal windows, and fits over the stay and the fixed bracket on the window frame.

To fit type 1, close the window and park the stay. Then position the lockable pin so that one of the stay holes locates over it, and mark the screw positions with a bradawl. Lift the stay aside and screw the pin in place. Then replace the stay and screw the lock-nut on to the pin to secure it, using the special key.

TIP . . .

If you don't want the option of locking the casement in the open position, retain the existing pin so that the stay

1. *Carefully mark the fixing holes and centrepunch them to stop the drill slipping*

3. *Screw the stop into place, remembering any gaskets which go between stop and frame*

2. *Drill fixing holes with window open to protect the casement. Take care to clear the glass edges*

4. *To operate, close the window and slide stop up to cockspur. Turn key to lock the window*

can be hooked on to it without the locking pin being used.

To fit type 2, close the window and slide the lock baseplate under the stay with the bolt extended to check that there is sufficient clearance. Holding the baseplate in position, withdraw the bolt so you can lift the stay out of the way and mark the positions of the fixing

screws. Attach the lock and check its action by using the key supplied to extend the bolt over the stay.

To fit a type 3 lock on a metal window, slip it over the stay and fixed bracket on the window frame and turn the locking screw with the key provided. Metal window stays have many bracket styles, so test a sample before buying locks for every window.

windows too; there are also special types for wood casements closing flush with their frames.

The simplest type to fit is the surface-mounted variety. Details vary from brand to brand, and manufacturers' individual fitting instructions should be followed carefully. A typical fitting sequence involves offering up the complete lock against the closed casement so its position can be marked on casement and frame. You then separate the two parts of the lock and screw each part into place with the fixing screws supplied. If the marking-out has been done accurately, the two parts should align perfectly when the window is closed. Small protective caps are often supplied to conceal the fixing screws when the lock has been installed. Check the position of the lock before you add these as they are difficult to remove.

With some models the bolt is pushed in to lock it (it is unlocked with a key); on others a key is used for both operations. One recently introduced model locks automatically when the window is closed – an obvious bonus.

The flush-fitting type usually has the lock body mounted on the casement and the keeper recessed into the frame over a mortise or drilled hole that accepts the bolt. This type is somewhat stronger than the surface-mounted variety, but needs careful installation and should not be fitted where the frame thickness is less than about 38mm (1½in). Again, follow the instructions carefully.

1. Fix threaded pin in place of existing plain one. Check stay holes line up with window shut

Fit a frame lock

There is a wide variety of frame locks available, all operating on the same principle of shooting a bolt into a keeper that is either surface-mounted or, for wood windows, recessed.

This type of lock offers a reasonable degree of security, especially if two are fitted near the opening corners of the casement rather than just one in the centre of the opening edge. There are different types for wood and metal windows. Some can be used on pivot

2. Close window firmly, fit stay over pin and screw on knurled nut to secure window

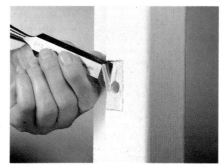

1. Cut recess with chisel. It should be deeper at the outside edge if the frame sides are bevelled

TIP . . .
With this type, position the keeper and cut the mortise (or drill the hole) first.

3. Alternative stay lock screws to frame – bolt shoots over stay to hold it in place

2. Screw plate in place – make sure it is square to window when shut. Adjust frame if necessary

3. Fix lock, taking its position from plate. Push bolt to lock. Add screw covers to complete

It's then easier to align and fit the surface-mounted lock body accurately on the opening casement.

Fitting a rack bolt

If you have reasonably substantial wooden casements and fanlights, you can fit small rack bolts, similar to those available for use on doors. The body of the bolt is recessed into the edge of the door, and a key-operated bolt is shot into a mating hole in the door frame. Ideally, two should be fitted to large casements for complete security.

Start by drilling a hole of the required diameter in the edge of the casement, after checking that the frame is wide enough to accept it. Then chisel out a shallow recess to accommodate the bolt faceplate and measure the distance between this and the keyhole on the lock body. Transfer this measurement to the frame, and carefully drill the keyhole through from the inner face to meet the bolt recess.

Slide the bolt body into the recess and secure it by driving in the two screws through its faceplate. Check that the key operates the bolt smoothly every time that you use it before adding the small keyhole plate on the inner face of the frame.

There is usually a small raised pip on the end of the bolt – operate the bolt so it leaves a corresponding mark on the frame. If there is no pip, put chalk or pencil lead on the end of the bolt instead. Drill a hole at this point for the

bolt – if one is supplied – it may need to be recessed into the frame.

Fitting a dual screw

If your frames aren't wide enough to accept a mortise rack bolt, you can fit a similar device called a dual screw instead. This has a surface-mounted block or bracket which is screwed to the frame, and a plate or recessed 'nut' on the casement itself; when the window is closed a locking nut is screwed into place through the frame block or bracket to hold the window closed. This type of bracket can also improve the fit of draughty windows.

To fit a dual screw lock, attach the plate to the closing face of the casement, or screw the recessed nut into a pre-drilled hole, according to type. Then close the window, position the block or bracket against the frame so the two parts align and screw it into place. Check the operation works with the special key provided.

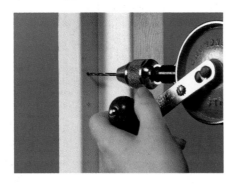
1. Drill pilot holes for fixing screws in casement first, then screw threaded pin in place

Fix bolt part of lock first and make the keeper recess after. Operate lock with toothed key.

2. Fix slotted bracket position from pin position and screw on. Tighten knurled nut to lock

Options

If you live in a high-risk area as far as burglaries are concerned, your windows may be vulnerable whatever locks and other security devices you fit. One option is to install window bars or a security grille – a made-to-measure metal frame that is fixed on the inside of the window reveal and still allows you to open and close the casement or fanlight (obviously, such a grille on the outside would prevent you from using the window for ventilation). The best place to go for bars and grilles is a locksmith or a specialist security firm. Various patterns are available, and many are comparatively unobtrusive in use. They certainly bring a greater peace of mind.

Concertina-type security gates, like those found on old-fashioned lifts, are the ultimate solution. They combine excellent security and a visible burglar deterrent with the advantage that you can push them back out of the way when you're at home. They are, however, very expensive. If you can't afford them and you're still worried about your home's security, join (or start up) a Neighbourhood Watch Scheme.

Window bars serve as permanent security. More expensive concertina types can be opened

BURGLAR ALARMS

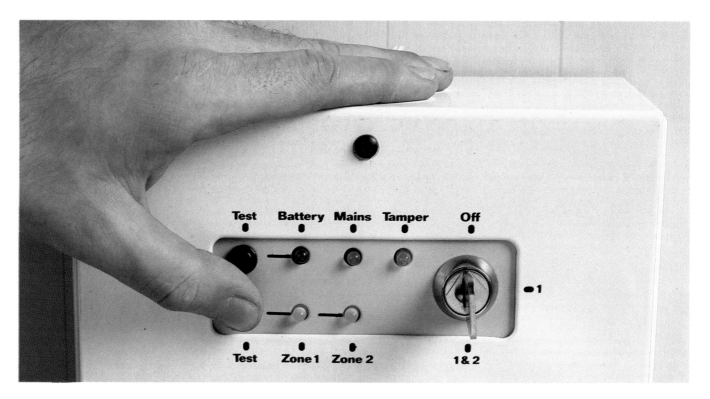

Home security is becoming increasingly important as burglary rates and insurance premiums rise year after year. Fitting locks and latches to all external doors and windows is the first, essential step to home security. For additional security (and peace of mind), consider installing a burglar alarm system.

If your home contains valuables you may be required by your insurance company to have a burglar alarm installed by a professional company. Follow their recommendations to ensure a suitable and trouble-free system. In other cases, there is a wide range of do-it-yourself alarms available.

Understanding the alarm system
Do-it-yourself alarms are easy to fit – little more trouble than wiring up a door-bell, for instance. But adding a burglar alarm to your house is not something to undertake lightly. It will cause bad relations with neighbours if it signals false alarms, and give you a false sense of security if it fails to react properly to unauthorized entry. So understanding how alarm systems work and how to install them correctly is essential if you plan to do-it-yourself.

An electrical alarm system consists of four main pieces of equipment:

A detection device (or devices); there are various types, but the most common is a simple electrical switch which switches either on or off when disturbed.

A signalling device; (usually simply electrical flex) this carries the electrical change noted by the detection device back to a control unit.

A control unit/panel; its main job is to monitor signals from the detection devices and, when it registers a change, to activate the warning device.

A warning device; usually bells mounted on the outside of the house, but can also take the form of an automatic warning telephone call to a police station or security centre.

Detection devices

Magnetic sensor
A magnetic sensor is the detection device most frequently used on doors and windows. A small electrical reed

Burglar alarms form circuits around the house. Sensors complete the circuit – break them and the alarm will sound.

switch is fitted to, say, the door frame, and a magnet is fitted to the door itself opposite the switch. When the door is closed, the magnet keeps the switch itself closed too. But when the door is opened, the magnet moves away from the switch, which also opens, signalling to the control unit which in turn (if the system is switched on), sets the alarm bells ringing.

This type of sensor is known as a closed-circuit type: it forms a closed electrical circuit while everything remains undisturbed, but breaking the circuit sets off the alarm. You can also fit open-circuit magnetic sensors: here, closing the circuit will set off the alarm.

Fitting a sensor
The simplest type to fit is a surface-mounted sensor, where both parts of the detector are glued or screwed to the face of the door or window and the frame. But a magnetic sensor can be beaten by a thief if he knows where it is sited – and a surface-mounted sensor

may well be clearly visible.

Recessed sensors are much harder to defeat because you can fit them anywhere along the opening parts of a door or window, and the thief won't know where. They are more trouble to fit – you have to drill holes in the door and frame – and, of course, they can be fitted only to wooden doors and windows.

Where to fit
Fit magnetic sensors to all downstairs doors and windows, and to any upstairs openings if these are easily accessible.

Pressure mats
A pressure mat provides a second line of defence if a burglar actually manages to break into your house. It is hidden underneath a carpet and sets off the alarm when someone treads on it. It is usually designed as an open-circuit detector – two sheets of metallic foil which are held slightly apart, and make contact only when trodden on.

Where to position
You can place pressure mats in front of particularly valuable items, such as the video recorder or a painting; on corridors leading to important areas of the house; on stairs to protect the upstairs; and in front of patio doors.

What to watch for
Although any detection device can be operated by accident, devices within the house itself are particularly susceptible to being set off unnecessarily – by family, visitors, or even the cat. So use them cautiously.

Movement detectors
Movement detectors are more versatile than other types: they react to movement over a wide area, not just to a door

Modern burglar alarms make use of a wide range of sensors, each tailored to detect a particular anomaly, be it vibration, movement, heat or unauthorized opening of doors or windows. Some also have a manually-controlled panic button in case an intruder does get into the house otherwise undetected, but all have a prominent external siren – still a powerful deterrent in urban areas.

being opened or a particular spot of carpet being trodden on. **Ultrasonic** and **microwave** types operate on the same principle – an emitter sends out a signal which covers a large area of a room and which is picked up by a receiver. Anyone moving in the area will upset the signal received and so set off the alarm. Microwave types can operate over a large distance, and even detect movement behind furniture and thin partitions: though this can be useful, it does mean you have to be careful how you site the unit and set it up. Ultrasonic types are easily fooled – not only pets, but even draughts and sudden changes in temperature may set them off.

A **passive infra-red** detector doesn't send out signals but 'reads' the pattern of infra-red radiation in the area: it senses the body heat of anyone moving within range.

Where to position
Movement detectors are fairly expensive, but one strategically sited may take the place of several magnetic

sensors and pressure mats, and will cut down on installation time.

Breaking-glass detectors
Breaking-glass detectors overcome some of the problems of magnetic sensors on opening windows, and can also be used to protect large fixed windows. One type consists of a length of thin metallic foil which sticks around the perimeter of the window. It is a closed circuit detector: breaking the window breaks the foil and opens an electrical contact, so setting off the alarm. However, it is possible for a large window to be broken without breaking the foil, so this type of detector may not prove secure enough in every case.

Another type is a vibration detector. This reacts to the jarring received when the window breaks and so is more likely to be set off wherever the window is smashed. But this type of ultra-sensitive detector is also more prone to false alarms – planes or heavy traffic are sometimes enough to vibrate the window and set off the alarm.

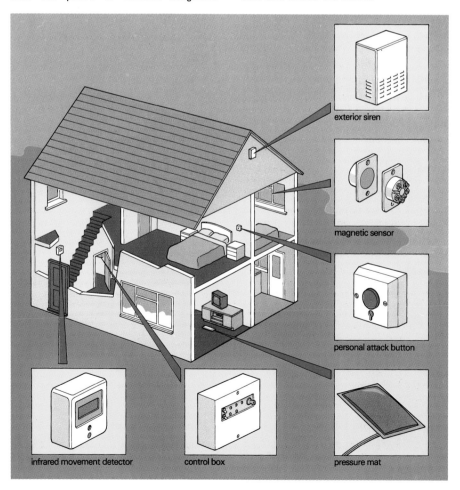

exterior siren

magnetic sensor

personal attack button

infrared movement detector

control box

pressure mat

Personal attack buttons

A personal attack button is simply a doorbell-type push-button that you press to set off the alarm whenever you think there might be danger. The device is comforting for elderly or infirm people who find it difficult to get to a telephone.

Where to position

Decide carefully where such 'panic buttons' may best be located – the usual site is near the bed so that you can easily raise the alarm at night. Other panic buttons could be located near the main external doors so that you have some means of summoning assistance if you answer the door to a visitor who then forces his way in.

Signalling devices

Electrical flex

The most common form of signalling device is simple electrical flex, connecting the detection devices to the control panel. Detection devices operate at around 12V and so lightweight 0.5A mains flex, or even in some cases bell wire, can be used. Thin cables are easy to lay and to hide.

Wiring up

You don't have to wire each detector individually to the control panel. For a neater, quicker job, several detectors can be looped together with a single cable feeding back to the control panel. But connect detectors separately to the panel if this would make wiring runs shorter. If you want to 'zone' your system (see page 21) you will need to wire detectors separately from each other on different zones. With normal two-wire cable you will also have to wire open-circuit detectors separately from closed-circuit ones.

If a thief can attack the wiring, there is a chance that he can overcome the alarm – by cutting the wires if they are feeding an open-circuit detector, or bridging them together if they are feeding a closed-circuit detector. A more secure system uses four-wire cable. Two of the wires feed the detectors in the normal way; the other two form a continuous monitor-circuit: cutting this circuit or trying to bridge it to the other wires will set off the alarm.

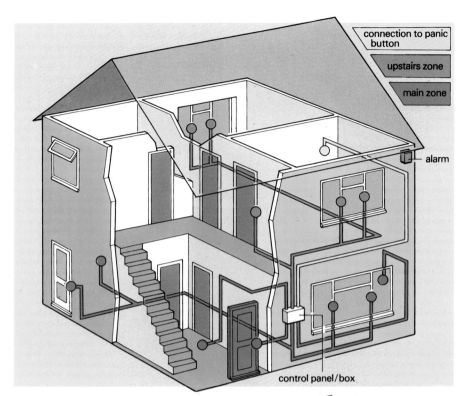

connection to panic button

upstairs zone

main zone

alarm

control panel/box

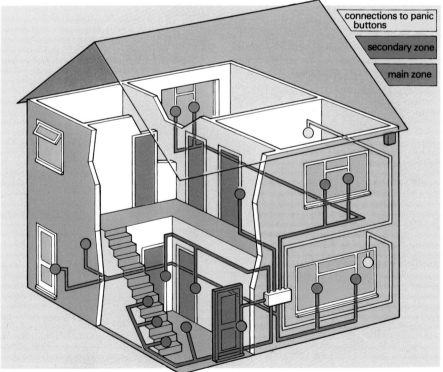

connections to panic buttons

secondary zone

main zone

Radio transmitter

A new development is the use of low-powered radio transmitters as the signalling device. Conventional types of detector can be used, but each one is connected to its own radio transmitter which signals coded digital information to a receiver in the control panel.

Two-zone alarm systems can be selectively activated to suit the situation. The top diagram shows circuitry which allows the downstairs only to be 'active'. The lower diagram shows a system whereby only entrypoints, both upstairs and down, are activated.

Advantages

The main advantage is the ease of installation, since no major wiring is involved (although some detectors, such as magnetic sensors, may still need a small length of cable running from them to the transmitter itself). Security may be improved too, since there is less chance of being able to tamper effectively with the system.

Control unit/panel

How it works

The control panel's main job is to take the signals from the detection devices, to monitor the system's circuits, and to raise the alarm when necessary. It also provides a power supply for the whole system, indicators to let you know what's happening, test facilities, and, of course, master on/off controls.

The panel may also contain its own tamper protection for extra security. Here, a microswitch within the casing is wired directly to the alarm – if a burglar tries to prise open the panel in order to disconnect the power, the switch triggers and the alarm is set off.

Most control panels treat the whole system as one – when it's switched on or off, all detectors are live or dead. But some offer variations. For example, tamper protection may be continuously live, so that tampering with the control panel at any time will set off the alarm.

Panic-button circuits may also be permanently live – if so, make particularly sure the buttons are out of the reach of children.

Convenient systems

Control panels may also split up the system into 'zones', each of which can be individually switched on or off. This enables you to have the system switched off in a section of the house that you're occupying and moving about in, yet operational in areas of the house that are vacant.

Operating the system

Switching the system on and off is not as simple as you might think. Once the alarm is set you must leave the house without any of the detection devices setting it off.

To make this possible, most control panels incorporate a delay – once the panel is set you have up to one minute to leave the house before the alarm is activated: during this period triggering detection devices won't have any effect. Similarly, when you enter the house there's a delay before the alarm rings: enough for you to get to the control panel and turn off the system.

Another method of allowing authorized entry and exit is to fit a bypass, or shunt switch, at the front door; there are various types. One is simply an externally-mounted on/off switch for the control panel – which is not a very secure arrangement. Another type disables the detector on the door or on the whole detection circuit.

Extra security

Better security is provided by fitting the door with a shunt lock. Here, the shunt switch mechanism is fitted into the front door lock, so that unlocking the door

---

Fitting a magnetic sensor

Fit recessed magnetic sensors to all ground floor wooden doors and windows. They are a cheap form of sensor and, with a little practice, are not at all difficult to fit.
● First check the gap between door and frame: a recessed sensor fits into the edge of the door (or window) and its frame – like a mortise door lock. The magnet may not be powerful enough to keep the reed switch closed if the gap is wider than about 6mm(¼in).
● Decide on a location for the sensor. Anywhere will do, but the further away from the hinge end the sensor is positioned, the more sensitive it will be to small movements of the door.
● Drill a hole in the edge of the door large enough to take the magnet part of the sensor. Sizes will vary from brand to brand, but might be about 30mm(1⅛in) deep and 15mm (⅜in) diameter. Aim for a press fit to prevent the sensor from loosening or being removed.

Most sensors have a flanged face: fitting this flush to the frame will make for a neater job and will help to hide it. A handyman's knife is probably the best tool for cutting the small recess required.
● Next, drill a corresponding hole in the frame opposite the one in the door to take the reed switch. Make sure there's enough depth for the switch and its wiring.
● The trickiest part of the job is

drilling the hole for the wiring. This has to pass from the bottom of the hole in the frame and out through the back of the frame at a point you can reach – removing the architrave may help you make a neat job. Use the smallest diameter hole that will take the cable and allow you a little bit of room.
● You will probably have to fiddle a bit with the cable to coax it into the hole and round the back of the frame. Connect

it to the switch, and push the switch into its hole, pulling on the cable to take up any slack. Hide the cable behind the architrave if you have removed this, then run it back to the control panel so it's hidden from view.
● It is a good idea to test your system stage by stage as you install it. So before fitting the sensors, wire up the control panel and, if necessary, the alarm bell.

1. Drill holes for sensor and rear wire entry.

2. Feed cable through rear of frame; connect sensors.

3. Attach wire discreetly to frames with cable clips.

disables the detector. Of course, you must ensure that the lock is of a high enough quality that it can't be picked easily or your system will be worthless.

Foiling the burglar

To make the system more secure, the on/off control on the panel is not a simple switch. Most are key-operated: though the lock may not be as sophisticated as the one on your front door it should take a minute or two to pick so that any thief who has managed to take advantage of an entry/exit delay and found your control panel should not be able to pick the lock and switch off the alarm before it sounds.

Handy push-buttons

Another system uses electronic push-buttons instead of a key: you have to tap in your own 'combination lock' number to switch the alarm on or off.

Power supply

An alarm system needs a secure power supply, otherwise it is easy to defeat and useless in power cuts. On the other hand, batteries may fail more easily than a mains supply. So most systems use both: a mains supply for the normal running, plus rechargeable batteries to cover power failures or deliberate sabotage. The unit switches to the batteries if the mains fail. An alternative is non-rechargeable batteries which may be the only power source or be simply a back-up.

Connecting a system

Connecting an alarm system to the mains is usually fairly easy. You could simply plug the control panel into a nearby power point, but even if the system has a battery back-up this is not very secure. A better method is to wire the unit via a switched, fused connection unit into a ring main or radial power circuit. For added protection, don't site the connection unit close to the control panel, and recess the cable from the unit to the panel into the wall.

And, for neatness if not for security, bury detection cables in the wall where they converge near the control panel.

Testing the system

It is essential to test facilities and indicators to check that the alarm system is working properly. A good alarm will, on switch-on, sound a buzzer (not the main alarm) if you have left any doors or windows open, or if any of the circuits are faulty. Lights may indicate where the fault is. Indicator lights should show you which zones are in operation, and warn you if the mains has failed or if battery power is low.

Warning devices

Boxed bell or siren

The warning device is the whole reason for having an alarm system. It must give adequate warning and be tamper-proof.

The most popular warning device is an external bell or siren in a metal box. This should be fixed where it is visible, but well out of reach of a thief. It can be protected in various ways.

First, all wires to it should pass directly from the box through the outside wall and into the house. Hide the wires carefully as they pass from the box back to the control panel. In addition, the bell can be self-actuating. This means it has its own power source and that any attempt to cut the wires to it will set it off. The bell box, like the control panel cabinet, may also have tamper protection fitted so that trying to prise it open will set off the alarm.

As well as an external alarm, some systems also have a small internal buzzer, operating a little before the main bell. In the case of false alarms it will give you time to get to the control panel before the main bell is set off.

Remote areas

An external alarm is of no use if there is no-one close by to hear it: country properties need a remote signalling device. This uses a telephone line, an autodialler and a tape recorder. The phone line is separate from your main line, and is designed for outgoing calls only. The autodialler can be set to dial wherever is most sensible – 999, your local police station, a neighbour, or your own work number. The tape recorder will then play a message to whoever picks up the phone.

Preventing false alarms

Almost all alarm calls are false alarms. If your system gives false alarms you won't be popular: the neighbours may refuse to investigate future calls, and so may the police. In the United Kingdom you could even find yourself being prosecuted under the Control of Pollution Act.
● To reduce the chance of false alarms:

Make sure all the family know how to operate the system and, in particular, how to enter and leave the house when the system is switched on. Make sure they keep out of areas protected by movement detectors when the system is switched on and the house is occupied.
● Impress on younger members that setting off the alarm deliberately is not a game. Check the system carefully before you set it. At least once a year check all wiring making sure there are no bare wires or loose contacts, and making sure that any batteries are fully charged.
● Tell the police that you have an alarm, and give them the names and addresses of a couple of neighbours you can

1. Fit control unit after bench-testing circuits.

2. Check system regularly for faulty connections.

trust with a set of keys and instructions for turning off and maybe resetting the alarm.

● If the alarm sounds before you can get to it to switch it off, adjust the timer setting.

HOME SAFETY

Is your home really safe? Or does it contain various hazards and dangers that could injure or even kill? Take time to do a safety check now, for the protection of yourself and your family.

Every year thousands of people die through accidents in the home. Even more are injured. The real tragedy is that most home accidents need never happen: they occur because people are careless and cannot be bothered to take safety seriously – even though it can be literally a matter of life and death.

Your home is so familiar to you that you are probably unaware of the many risks contained in every room. But they are there just the same. Not only does it make sense to carry out a safety survey regularly; it is also important to develop safety habits for the day-in-day-out well-being of everyone concerned. Most accidents occur because people – knowingly or unknowingly – take risks like rushing down the stairs at night without turning on the light or slicing vegetables straight into a saucepan rather than on to a chopping board first.

Kitchen hazards

So many avoidable disasters happen in the kitchen. For instance, just reaching up to get something out of a cupboard – positioned too high for comfort – could start a chain-reaction mishap if the chair you are standing on slips or something falls out of the cupboard on to your head.

Always use proper household steps for reaching heights: they are more stable than stools and chairs and, because they are higher, they prevent the need to over-reach and balance precariously. It is also important to fit wall storage at a height within normal reach, especially if it is in everyday use. High cupboards and shelves should be reserved for items that are only needed occasionally. Do not stretch to cupboards over a cooker when any of the burners or hot plates are turned on.

Children and safety

Cookers are always a source of high risk, not just from the oven heat, or the knobs that can be reached and turned on by small children, or burners which are still hot though not red enough to show, but from the cooking pans themselves. Handles should be moved out of harm's way, not left over a source of heat so that when picked up they will be unexpectedly hot. Nor should handles be left poking out where someone could catch a sleeve and bring the contents of the pan – often boiling – scattering dangerously everywhere.

Electrical appliances should never be near water – keep the food mixer away from the sink, and check that work surfaces are firm and steady if any cutting is to be done.

Commonsense precautions

Newly-washed wet or highly polished floors are a potential danger for anyone walking into the room if no warning has been given. A moment's thought is all that is needed to prevent a mishap.

Glass doors should be made of the specially toughened glass available today, especially if there are children in the house who might fall and hurt themselves. Of course, children can always be a liability in a home and a little extra thought can save them from serious accidents in the future. Common sense and an awareness of possible danger areas are generally all that are required.

Lastly, be sure to keep a well-stocked First Aid kit in the house (see First Aid section) and keep the telephone numbers of hospitals and local doctors readily at hand.

On the following pages we look at common accidents that take place around the home and in the garden. After reading the safety advice it is a good idea then to refer to the First Aid section so that you will know what to do if an accident occurs in your home.

SAFE AS HOUSES

However careful you and your family are in your home it's all too easy to trip and fall accidentally. In fact, falls account for more injuries and deaths than any other type of home accident. Help to prevent falls, slips and trips by following these safety rules:

● Check your lighting. Many falls result from poor lighting: people cannot see where they are going. This is especially true in porches and on stairways, so ensure that these areas are well lit. For stairs and hallways, install return switches so that you can turn the light on and off wherever you are.
● Highly-polished floors and loose or damaged floor coverings can also cause falls, so on wooden, tiled or vinyl floors use a non-slip polish. Attach non-slip backings to rugs and mats: check regularly that fitted carpets have not worked loose.
● Wipe up bathroom and kitchen spills immediately, before anyone has a chance to slide or tumble.
● Do not leave things lying about on the floor – particularly in dimly-lit areas where they could be fallen over.
● Do not let long electric flexes or telephone leads trail across the floor.

Electrical hazards

Most electrical accidents can be avoided if you take note of the following safety information.

WIRING If the wiring circuit in your home is over 25 years old it should be

checked for faults. Even a modern circuit should be tested regularly, about every five years. Always have checks and subsequent rewiring carried out by approved contractors.

APPLIANCES All electrical equipment must conform to strict safety standards. Make sure that any appliance you buy carries the relevant safety label. If you buy second-hand equipment, have it checked before use.

PLUGS When buying plugs, check that they have an approved label. Then make sure that you wire them up securely and correctly thus: brown (live), blue (neutral), green/yellow (earth). Also fit the appropriate fuse: a 3 amp fuse for up to 750 watts; a 13 amp fuse for over 750 watts. A plate on the appliance indicates wattage. Switch off and unplug all appliances when they are not in use, especially at night.

FLEXES These must also be in good condition; replace worn or damaged ones immediately. If a flex is not long

enough, fit a new one rather than joining on an extra length. If you do join two ends of flex, use a proper connector, not insulating tape. Avoid long flexes trailing across the floor: if there is no power point where you need it, have one installed. Similarly, fit extra power points rather than running three or four appliances off a single point.

FOLLOW INSTRUCTIONS Always use appliances according to the manufacturer's instructions. If anything, however slight, appears to be wrong, switch off and unplug at once.

WATCHPOINTS Above all, remember that electricity and water do not mix:
● Do not handle an appliance, plug, switch or flex with wet hands.
● Do not stand on a newly-washed floor when ironing.
● Do not use the vacuum on wet patches on floors or carpets.
● Do not empty or fill a kettle with the current still switched on.
● Never take a mains-operated appliance into the bathroom.

Beware poison!

Your home contains various poisons in the shape of medicines, cleaning fluids, garden chemicals and DIY materials. Treat all such substances with respect and carefully follow instructions for use and storage.

Apart from the obvious precaution of keeping all poisons locked away from children and pets, make sure you use tightly-closed and well-labelled jars and bottles; this is especially important if you are transferring the contents of a bulk container into a small one.

Never transfer medicines from their original containers. When you have finished taking a medicine (including tablets), either return any leftovers to a chemist or flush them down the toilet.

Garden safety

Outdoor accidents – particularly when using electrical gardening equipment – are a common cause of injury, and even death. Follow these basic safety rules for outdoor safety.

● Check your garden and overall outdoor area. Uneven paving, cracked doorsteps, overgrown paths and slippery leaves can all cause falls.

● If you have electrical equipment, such as lawn mowers or hedge trimmers, follow the operating instructions carefully and always plug the appliance into a socket protected by a residual current device (RCD) or into an adaptor containing an RCD. This cuts off the current immediately if you touch any live part. Never use electric mowers on wet grass. With other electrical tools, if there is heavy dew or the ground is damp, wear rubber boots for increased protection. Whatever the weather, if you are using a sharp tool, do not wear open or flimsy sandals.

● Cutting grass leads to more accidents than any other gardening activity. Safety guidelines, for both petrol-driven and electric machines, are:
– clear the lawn of stones and twigs before you start
– always move the lawn mower away from you and across slopes rather than pushing the mower up them
– turn off the mower to adjust or unclog blades and also when you leave it – even if only for a few moments
● Do not leave tools – either electrical or hand – lying around in the garden where people can fall over or on to them. Always carry tools point down.
● Keep fertilizers, weed killers and any other chemicals safely locked up.
● if a greenhouse window breaks,

Accidents with gas

Gas can cause explosions, so keep a general look-out for leaks. If you do suspect a leak, extinguish all naked lights such as cigarettes. Open doors and windows and inform the emergency service – but don't use your own phone as this could ignite the gas. (Also, do not use electrical switches.) For peace of mind make sure you know where the main gas tap is and how to turn it off.

● When buying gas appliances, look for approved safety labels, have appliances fitted by a registered installer and serviced regularly.

● Remember that gas appliances need ventilation, so check that flues, ventilators and air bricks do not become blocked or obstructed.

immediately remove and safely dispose of the shattered glass.

● Outdoor accidents happen during decorating. Remember these tips:
– make sure ladders are well maintained and stably positioned
– use blowlamps carefully – pointed away from yourself and other people
– make sure that power tools are working properly and have adequate extension leads
– wear safety goggles and gloves
– store toxic materials safely.

Cuts and scratches

Cuts should be taken seriously. A careless habit that causes just a scratch today might lead to an infected finger, or worse, tomorrow.

In the kitchen, always slice food downwards on to a flat surface and put knives away after use – ideally in a wood block. Make sure that your tin opener works smoothly; do not prise up the opened lid with your fingers, and, as soon as an opened can is empty, push the lid back inside and throw it away. Take care when sewing: if you drop a pin or a needle, pick it up at once (a magnet is helpful). To clear up broken glass or china, always use a brush – not your bare hands – and wrap the fragments in thick newspaper before disposing of them in the dustbin.

DIY SAFETY

Left: Always ensure that ladders are firmly secured, especially when they are not based on ground level.

'Act on impulse, repent at leisure' is the maxim that should be engraved on all DIYers' tool kits, for according to Consumer Safety Unit research, most accidents occur because people do not take sensible precautions.

The Consumer Safety Unit, part of the Department of Trade and Industry, has been producing annual reports on home accidents (with DIY accidents included) since 1976. Further, more detailed, studies have been carried out, looking at particular problems and specific accidents to evaluate how much the equipment was to blame, and to recommend changes in design or make suggestions about safer use of equipment.

The latest figures show that most accidents occur when the following tools and equipment are used in the home, without due care and attention:
● Non-domestic knives
● Electric drills
● Straight blade saws
● Circular saws
● Stepladders
● Leaning ladders

In the analysis of these accidents, two factors predominated:
● People tend not to take precautions when doing DIY. They neglect to use eye protectors, gloves and dust masks.
● Material or equipment is not properly secured in a vice or Workmate; far too often a hand, a foot or another part of the body is used to hold the object to be worked on in position.

Hand tools

Non-domestic knives, hammers, mallets, chisels, screwdrivers and saws are the hand-tools most in use when DIY accidents resulting in cuts or punctures to the skin occur. In most cases, one or more of the following safety points were being ignored by the DIYer.

Safety points: hand tools
● Try to always use the correct tool for the job rather than making do with what is at hand. A screwdriver should be slightly wider than the slot in the screw and not used as a chisel or lever. Pincers and pliers must not be used to undo nuts. Spanners should be the correct size for the nut and the jaws must not be worn.
● A blunt tool is much more likely to slip than a sharp one. Well-stored tools are less likely to deteriorate and cause injuries. Fit guards over sharp edges.
● When using tools keep your spare hand and your body out of the way. When possible, secure material with clamps or a vice. Always move the tool away from, rather than towards, your body. When cutting vinyl or carpet use a straightedge with a right-angled side, not a bevelled edge, or the knife will tend to ride up it. Don't use excessive pressure. Change blades often.
● When buying DIY tools choose the best quality goods you can afford. Cheap tools are usually of poor quality and will chip more easily and tend to shatter or break in use. Hold the tool in your hand for a few moments to check both the balance and the comfort of the handle before you buy.

Power tools

By far the greatest number of power-tool accidents involve drills or saws. Most damage is received by hands, particularly fingers and thumbs, but flying debris thrown into unprotected eyes is also quite common, and there have even been cases of electrocution. In most cases studied by the Consumer Safety Unit the accidents could have been avoided if the user had been properly protected and the work had been well secured.

Drills

In a study of 44 accidents involving electric drills, the work was secured by a vice or grip in only six cases; in most it was held by the user's hand, body or foot. The risk of accidents appears to be greatest when drilling metal where, quite often, the drill bit breaks. Out of nine cases where fragments flew into the drill-users' eyes, six involved metal and the other three brick or tile. Most accidents involving drill use occurred where work was being done at, or above, shoulder height.

Safety points: power tools

● Use eye protectors, particularly when drilling metal, brick or tiles. Always secure work in a vice or a Workmate, if possible.
● Select the right size and type of drill bit and make sure that it is sharp – a blunt bit is far more likely to slip. Use a centre punch to make a slight depression before starting. Select the correct drill speed for the work. Prepare work by drilling a pilot hole before you drill the main one.

Circular saws

Among accidents involving hand-held and table-mounted saws, powered blades cause the most damage to hands. Sawdust or chips of wood can be thrown into the eyes of portable saw users. Only in about one-third of accidents involving hand-held saws is the work clamped or held in a vice.

Safety points

● The blade should be sharp, suitable for the material being cut, and the saw should be powerful enough to cope with the job in hand.
● Use eye protectors.
● Don't hold the work by hand. Use a push stick with a table-mounted saw.
● When buying, borrowing or hiring a circular saw, check whether the switch could be inadvertently operated. In some of the accidents mentioned above, the switch was activated by someone leaning forward to adjust the work.
● Check the stopping time of the blades; some continue revolving for an excessive time after switching off.
● Look at the guard – is it easy to retract, easy to clean, likely to stick, suitable for different cutting jobs?

Chain saws

Most chain-saw accidents occur because the user is operating the saw with only one hand and steadying the work or holding a branch with the other. Other accidents involving chain saws are due to unexpected events, like the user slipping, losing balance due to unstable or inadequate support, or the saw becoming trapped, bouncing or skidding on the work.

Safety points: saws

● Make sure anything you stand on is completely stable.
● Always work with both hands on the saw and with your body evenly balanced on both feet.
● Keep the chain correctly tensioned and well oiled.
● When buying, borrowing or hiring a chain saw, first read the instructions very carefully on how to use it.
● Check to see whether there is a delay in the saw chain coming to rest after release of the trigger.

● Buy a model with a chainbrake and make sure that it stops the chain immediately.
● Choose a design with low-profile safety chains with profiled guard links.
● Check the handle for good balance.

Angle grinders

No specific research has been carried out on accidents involving angle grinders, but the inevitable grit that is created by this kind of work means that eye protectors must always be worn. A dust mask that protects mouth and nose should also be used. Car refinishing suppliers are likely to have the best

It is easy to feel safe if you wear protective gloves while using a circular saw, but they are no match for a sharp blade rotating at high speed. If you wear safety gloves when operating machinery, they must fit well or they could catch in moving parts.

choice – do not settle for the cheaper masks that are only intended for use where dust is a nuisance rather than a hazard. Protective gloves are a further necessity in most cases.

It is also advisable to use a circuit breaker with any power tool. Although the number of instances of electrocution is small, it remains one of the commonest causes of death as opposed to injury.

Ladders

Most accidents involving leaning ladders and stepladders are the result of falls due to over-reaching and over-balancing. Bad footwear also contributes, and so does failure to secure the ladder in such a way that it does not slip. Stepladders can be dangerous if not fully opened, or if not placed at right angles to the work. Frequently, a ladder will slip because it is not standing on firm, level ground.

Safety points: leaning ladders

● Use a ladder of the right height for the job. Angled against the wall, the ladder top should reach 1m(3ft) above the highest point to be worked on. For every metre of ladder height the base should be 250mm(10in) away from the wall and extensions should overlap by 2-4 rungs depending on the ladder length (up to 5m(16½ft) minimum for 1½ rungs, over 5m(16½ft) for 3½ rungs).
● Before using, check for missing steps or rungs and for loose rungs (if they can be moved or twisted by hand they are loose). Replace if necessary.
● Stand the ladder on a firm base. On soft earth, put down a board and make sure that it is level and secure.
● Wear well-fitting shoes with a firm sole and check that the soles are free of mud before beginning to climb.
● If possible, lash the top of the ladder to something secure by the uprights, not the rungs. Get someone to foot the ladder at the base while you do this.
● Use a bracing board at windows and secure all doors that could open on to the ladder.
● Do not overreach, do not climb higher than the third rung from the top, and do not use a ladder in a high wind.

Safety points: stepladders

● Where possible, place the ladder at right angles to the work and always open it out to the fullest extent.
● Do not use the top tread unless there is a handrail support above it.
● Do not stand on the rear of the steps or share the steps with someone else.

Chemicals

Chemicals are often potentially dangerous. They can be flammable, toxic, corrosive or irritant. Check the information on the product label when buying, and get to know the significance of the warning symbols. Many accidents involving chemicals happen because potentially harmful substances are not kept out of the reach of children, or hazard warnings are disregarded and insufficient precautions are taken.

Left: Most domestic accidents occur because people do not take adequate precautions during DIY work.

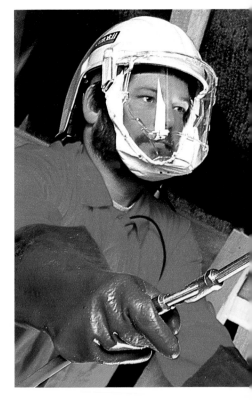

Safety points: chemicals

● Keep chemicals out of the reach of children at all times.
● Carefully read and follow all the instructions supplied by the manufacturer.
● Keep other adults, children and animals out of the room or area where chemicals are being used.
● Do not eat or smoke in the area where chemicals are being used.

Flammable (no symbol required) Paints, varnishes, wood dyes, preservatives, turpentine, white spirit and adhesives containing petroleum mixtures all come into this category. Do not use them near any source of ignition, whether flames or sparks; clean up debris and dispose of it safely – not by burning! Beware of inflammable vapours that collect at ground level.
Toxic Chemicals which are harmful if inhaled or absorbed through the skin, or if they contaminate food.

Left: Using chemicals in a confined space without wearing goggles, mask and gloves would be courting disaster, yet many people do just that. Far better to call in professionals.

● Never rely on ventilation as the sole protection, even out in the open.
● Use protective clothing, gloves and eye protectors, plus dust masks where appropriate.
● Wash well after using chemicals, including hair and clothing.
● Keep a bucket of water handy to flush chemicals away if you spill any or if there is contact with the skin.
● Be especially careful about wood preservatives which can be present in the air in an enclosed space for weeks after they have been applied to wood.

General diy safety

Although the statistics compiled by the Consumer Safety Unit show that most domestic accidents occur because people take inadequate precautions during DIY and routine maintenance work around the house, there are other home activities that often lead to serious accidents.

A great many accidents are caused by faulty electrical wiring or by incorrectly earthed appliances. Touching electric cords, wires or fixtures is perfectly safe in most cases, but if you do so while your hands, feet or shoes are damp, you may be inviting disaster. If your cords and plugs show frayed or cracked insulation it is only a matter of time before someone in your home, quite possibly a child, sustains a serious shock or even suffers electrocution. Unless you know exactly what you are doing, and are fully aware of the dangers involved, you should entrust any major electrical work or repairs to an approved electrician.

Nearly half of all the accidental deaths that occur at home are caused by falls. Many people who climb on chairs, boxes and other makeshift supports to reach high places, lose balance and crash on to the floor or against a piece of furniture. A stepladder should be an essential piece of equipment in every home.

A high proportion of accidents also take place during vehicle maintenance, and a smaller number during gardening. This indicates that car repairs and gardening are not taken sufficiently seriously and require much more care before work starts. All the tools and power connections should be checked thoroughly before a job begins, and the tools should always be appropriate for the job. It is a good idea to practice with a new tool before attempting to use it. A car engine should never be run in a closed garage, where a lethal dose of carbon monoxide gas can build up in no time at all. Installing home smoke detectors is always a good idea.

Remember, it takes no more than a few minutes to check and double check safety precautions, and if you're at all worried about any aspect of a DIY job – don't do it; ask for expert advice.

Very toxic A chronic health risk if inhaled or if the chemical penetrates the skin.
Harmful Of limited health risk in above situations. It is essential to work in a well ventilated area and to ensure that the product is not splashed on skin or into eyes.
Corrosive Contains chemicals which are strongly acidic or strongly alkaline and (EEC directive) 'may, on contact with living tissues, destroy them'. Again, you should make sure that both skin and eyes are protected from splashes.

Irritant Defined as chemical 'which through immediate or prolonged or repeated contact with the skin or mucous membrane can cause inflammation'. Good protective clothing, eye protectors and well ventilated surroundings are all important.
Explosive Any chemical or a mixture of chemicals capable of changing rapidly from solid or liquid form to gas and expanding violently.
Oxidising Releases oxygen in some conditions. Corrosive and may burst into flames.

FIRE PREVENTION

Fire in the home is a major hazard, yet a few simple precautions, costing little, will minimize the risk.

Fire is the product of three things: air, combustible material and ignition. Take away any one of the three and the fire will not occur. One simple precaution, therefore, is to have as few combustible materials as possible around the house. Be aware of the flammability of new upholstery (especially foam), cladding or wall-coverings.

Smoke hazard
Smoke is a far greater killer than flame. Often, victims are overcome by smoke and toxic fumes before they are even aware of what is happening. Smouldering polyurethane foam, for example, gives off lethal fumes and even some

heating appliances can give off carbon monoxide – a highly poisonous gas – if ventilation is insufficient or the appliance malfunctions. It is therefore essential to buy approved appliances (look for the ASTA and Kite marks and the BS number). Make sure that all appliances are properly installed, maintained and used. Never block off fixed vents, such as air bricks.

Safety in the kitchen
The kitchen is the most dangerous room in the house. By far the commonest cause of domestic fire is a chip pan or deep-fat drier bursting into flames.
   You can avoid this by observing a few simple rules:
● Don't fill the pan more than half full
● Don't let it get so hot it smokes
● Never leave it unattended.

If the pan or frier does catch light:
● Turn off the heat underneath it
● Cover the flames with a lid or a damp (not wet) tea towel or a fire blanket
● Leave it to cool for at least 30 minutes
● Don't try to pick up the pan or put out the fire with water.

Flammable materials
Avoid polystyrene tiles in the kitchen, even fire-retardant ones. Elsewhere, glue them firmly on a bed of adhesive — not just dabs — and paint with water-based paint, not gloss.
   Butane and propane are highly flammable and spare containers should not be stored in the house. If you run an appliance off one of these bottled gases, make sure that it does not leak and is shielded from heat.

What if you smell gas?
If you smell gas, turn off the mains, open doors and windows and check appliances for leaks. Don't turn any electrical switches on or off for fear of causing a spark, and, of course, stub out cigarettes and avoid naked lights. If it is a mains leak, telephone and inform the Gas Board immediately.

Sitting-room safety
The sitting-room can combine soft furnishings and open fires – both points to watch. Most of the block foam that is now so popular for stuffing furniture, is highly flammable and also gives off poisonous fumes once alight. Be aware of the danger and take care not to expose it to any kind of direct heat from a radiant or open fire. Keep ashtrays away too. And, when buying new foam-filled furniture or foam-filling for DIY furniture, always opt for flame-resistant products. To avoid accidental fires starting in a much-used family sitting-room, follow these basic safety precautions:
● If you re-upholster your sofa, choose a fire-resistant fabric if possible. Look for the Kite mark.
● Faulty electrical wiring is at the root of thousands of domestic fires each year. It is essential that all wiring circuits are correctly fitted and well maintained. Check circuits at least every five years.
● If a flex is too short then replace it; don't cobble it to another piece. If you

have to make a temporary join, use purpose-made connector blocks with the correct amp rating.

● Overloaded sockets catch fire all too easily. No more than one appliance should be plugged into one socket.

● Avoid an outcrop of adaptors by installing an extra double socket.

● Avoid trailing flex, especially under rugs or carpets.

● All electrical fittings should be regularly serviced and electrical appliances, such as televisions, stereos and heaters, should be properly ventilated and disconnected when not in use.

● Never fit a time-switch to a radiant electric-bar heater.

● If you are installing a new open fire, don't lay the hearthstone directly onto a timber joist as the heat could char it or even set it alight.

● Make sure that all chimneys and flues are properly fitted, and sweep the chimney regularly (see page 33).

● Always put an all-round, fine-mesh guard on the fire when there are children or old people in the room and when you leave the fire at night.

● Never hang a mirror over an open fire. It encourages people to stand too close and risk setting fire to clothes.

Staircase and hallway safety

The hallway and stairs are your main escape route, so keep these areas clear of clutter. Don't position a portable heater – particularly a paraffin heater –

Every room in the average home is full of potential dangers; take time to check and see what can be done about them

in a hallway, or indeed anywhere that it could be knocked over or where it is in a strong draught. Never carry a portable heater when it is alight.

The cupboard under the stairs tends to be used as a repository for all kinds of junk, but if a fire starts here, it will almost certainly engulf the stairs and cut off a possible escape route before you have time to get out.

Store flammable liquids and combustible materials somewhere other than under the stairs – preferably out of doors. If you don't have any outside storage, use a well-ventilated cupboard away from the stairs, in a corner opposite a door so you can retreat if a fire does start. Ventilation is essential because flammable vapours in a confined space could explode if a spark – from a lit cigarette, for example – were to come into contact with them.

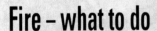

Fire – what to do

If a fire starts despite all your precautions, it's important to act correctly. Delay and confusion can kill. Follow these steps.

● **Close the door of the room where the fire is, to contain the smoke and flames as much as possible.**
● **Alert everyone in the house and get them out by the safest route. Don't use the lift.**
● **Alert neighbours and call the Fire brigade yourself.**
● **If you can do so in safety, close doors and windows to cut down draughts that may fan the flames.**

If, once you have got everyone else to safety, you feel that it is safe to fight the fire, proceed with caution. Only the smallest fires should be tackled by unequipped and untrained people. Remember that in city areas, it usually takes the Fire brigade less than five minutes to reach you.

If you believe that you have extinguished a fire, move any burnt furniture out of doors, but still call the Fire brigade to make sure it really is out. A doused fire can spring up again, even hours later.

Fire spreads rapidly once it gets hold in a room. A few flames can quickly turn into a raging inferno.

Fire safety in the bedroom
Follow these simple safety rules:
● Smoking – especially in bed – is a common cause of domestic fires. The Fire brigade have a simple answer – don't do it.
● Electric blankets, like all appliances, need to be properly used and maintained; they are among the five most frequent fire causes. Some types should be turned off before you get into bed, because they should not have weight put on them, and have them serviced at least every three years.
● Don't dim a bedside light by draping a cloth over it; buy a low-wattage bulb instead, or fit a dimmer switch.
● Bedroom windows may well prove to be your only escape route if a fire breaks out downstairs when you are sleeping. You must, therefore, be able to open them. If you are fitting double-glazing, don't use fixed panes.

Chip pans should never be left heating on the stove, not even for a few moments

● If you lock your windows or internal doors at night, make sure that keys are placed nearby and that you can find them in the dark.

Children's bedrooms
A child's bedroom has a way of attracting clutter. Make sure that discarded clothes and toys cannot come into contact with heaters, light bulbs or other heat sources. Never leave a candle as a night light and make sure that fires have proper fine-mesh guards.

Attic safety watchpoints
Never leave a heater on in the attic to thaw out pipes – it's easy to forget that it's there. Lag all the pipes properly to insulate them instead.

Avoid storing flammable material or liquids in the attic. Fires in attics are often not spotted until they are well established, and they are about the hardest for the Fire brigade to fight.

Garage and workshop safety
By law, you must have a self-closing, fire-resistant door between the garage

All kitchens should have a properly serviced fire extinguisher, or fire blanket near the cooker.

and the house if there is direct access.

If you store petrol in the garage, the garage must, by law, be well ventilated and have direct access to the open air; you must also have suitable firefighting equipment to hand. The maximum you may store is two 2-gallon containers – plus whatever is in the fuel tank of your car or motorbike.

Piles of woodshavings and oily rags make ideal tinder, so keep your workshop tidy. Don't rig up makeshift wiring for power tools or lighting.

Doing DIY safely

An average 1500 domestic fires per year are caused by blowlamps. Sudden flares and blow-outs may take you by surprise, so keep some wet sacking handy in the workshop, and never leave a lit blowlamp unattended.

There are two types of flame-retardant paint available: intumescent paint, which expands when heated to form an insulating layer, and antimony-based paint, which gives off a vapour when heated and prevents air from reaching the surface, so stopping it burning. It's worth considering when redecorating the kitchen.

Sleep safely

At night, empty ashtrays, make sure any fire is dampened down and guarded and close all internal doors downstairs. Then, if a fire does start, it will be contained in one room. A hardwood door should contain a fire for about 30 minutes – more than enough to get everyone to safety and call the Fire brigade.

Fire warning systems

A recent survey suggested that 40 per cent of deaths in domestic fires could

Sweeping a chimney

Chimneys should be swept at least once and preferably twice a year, particularly if you are burning wood. Otherwise soot, tar and creosote will collect in the flue, creating a considerable fire hazard. Also, tar deposits can penetrate the brickwork and wreck surrounding decorations.

Brushes can be bought or hired and you can also hire special chimney vacuuming equipment. Whether you hire or buy, make sure that the brush has polypropylene or natural bristles. Wire bristles can scratch the flue liner, creating an ideal foothold for tar and creosote deposits. Wire brushes may also damage brick chimneys, leaving cracks for the smoke to escape.

You can also buy chemical cleaning agents, which you sprinkle on the fire. The smoke contains a gas that reacts with the soot to form a flaky scale that does not hold to the sides of the flue.

If you decide to brush the chimney – the least expensive and perhaps most reliable method – take care that you do not damage the flue or the chimney pot. Wear your oldest clothes – you are bound to get very dirty. Keep children and pets well out of the way.
● Work from the fireplace up rather than from the roof down.
● Close all doors and windows to prevent soot flying around.
● Cover all the furniture and carpets in the room with plastic sheeting and the fire surround with newspaper and masking tape, to protect them from soot.
● Remove the grate and fireback (if removable) and open the throat restrictor. (This is the hinged metal flap set across the flue to regulate the flow of air up the chimney – not all chimneys have them.)
● Push the first section of rod through a polyethylene sheet,

and then connect the brush.
● Push the brush up through the throat restrictor flap, being careful not to tear the sheet. Tape the sheet to the fire surround and weight the bottom to catch any falling soot.
● Work the brush head up and down a few times, then add the next rod section, turning the rods clockwise each time to avoid unscrewing ones you've already fixed. Repeat this pattern of movement until you have added all the sections needed to reach the top of the chimney stack. Work slowly and methodically, to avoid a sudden cascade of soot caused by an artificial down-draught. Also, be careful not to

push the brush up so hard that you knock the cowling off.
● When the brush reaches the top of the chimney, the pressure on the handle will decrease. Now you can slowly bring the brush back down, remembering to turn it clockwise. Detach rod sections as they appear.
● Once you have brought the brush back down, detach the polyethylene sheet with great care and scoop up the soot and debris. Take it outside in buckets covered with damp cloths.
● If there is a smoke shelf at the top of the fireback, it will have collected a great deal of dust and soot. Sweep it clean by hand with a small brush.

Push rod through polythene sheeting and fit brush

Work brush up chimney, adding rods as required

Cover the carpets with newspaper before you start

Safety for children

Everyone knows not to let children play with matches, but this is still the third most common cause of domestic fires. Make sure that they can't find them when you're out of the house.

Think about flammability when shopping for your children's nightclothes. Nightdresses and pyjamas are covered by British Standard regulations, but dressing gowns are not. Look for the Kite mark and choose cotton or 100 per cent brushed nylon.

Make sure, too, that your children know what to do if a fire starts. If the stairs are on fire, the heatwave from the landing as they open their bedroom door may knock them backwards and even set them alight. Work out a family fire drill and make sure that all children old enough to understand know how to behave, what to do if you can't reach them and how to phone 999. Planning coolly before the event can make the difference between life and death.

be avoided by installing an early-warning system. There are two types of fire detector available: heat detectors and smoke detectors.

● Heat detectors are largely unsuitable for domestic use, since they ignore

For maximum safety, keep fire extinguishers handy and fit smoke detectors

heavy smoke and only react once the heat is intense.

● Smoke detectors are a sensible investment. There are two varieties: ionization – better at detecting blazing fires – and photoelectric, which is better for smouldering fires. Some models use both principles.

The ionization type uses a tiny radioactive source to ionize the air inside it, allowing an electric current to flow. Smoke reduces the current, which triggers the alarm.

Photoelectric detectors pass a beam of light close to a photoelectric cell. Smoke scatters the light onto the cell and the alarm sounds.

Both emit a piercing buzz or wail, designed to wake you from the deepest slumber. The best models have a 'low battery warning' noise and/or light and a built-in safety light.

Choosing a safe site

The detector should be close enough to the living-room and kitchen (but not *in* the kitchen), to detect a fire early on, and the alarm should be able to wake you. If your house is large or your doors thick; install two or more interconnected detectors.

Firefighting equipment

A wide range of firefighting equipment is available but the London Fire Brigade point out that, in untrained hands, it can be a danger. Believing that you can fight the fire may make you delay evacuating the house or calling the Fire brigade.

A fire blanket is a fibreglass sheet which can be useful for dousing sudden

All fire extinguishers need to be properly maintained and correctly used. Read the instructions carefully.

Building regulations

If you are planning any major structural alterations, you must be aware of the Building Regulations. If you are planning to knock through a wall, for example, you must ensure that it is not needed for fire resistance. An attic conversion means that many more fire regulations will apply to your house.

Any house with a storey more than 6.25m (20ft) above ground level should have a protected stairway leading directly to a street exit, connecting to all floors. There should also be an additional means of second floor escape, via a dormer or roof window.

Open-plan living creates greater risks than traditional room plans, since fire will spread far more quickly without internal doors and dividing walls. If a stairway to an upper floor starts in an open-plan area, you should fit a fire-resistant, self-closing door at the head of the stairs and provide an alternative route out from the storey above.

Safety lighting should be installed on little-used stairways and other escape routes, and should come on automatically if the mains power fails, or else every night at dusk. Both safety lighting and fire alarm circuits should be isolated from other domestic circuits. Many of these regulations apply only to large blocks of flats, but there are plenty of precautions that the ordinary householder can take.

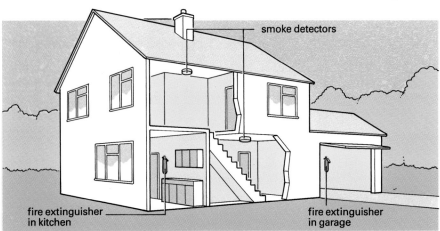

smoke detectors

fire extinguisher in kitchen

fire extinguisher in garage

flare-ups such as a chip-pan fire. A fire blanket can also be used to wrap around someone whose clothing has caught fire.

There are five types of fire extinguisher: water, carbon dioxide, halon, dry powder and foam.

● Water is fine for most fires but is dangerous if used on a fire involving fat or electricity.

● Carbon dioxide is suitable for flammable liquids and electrical fires.

● Halon is the right choice for all fires except those involving metals.

● General-purpose dry powder is good on most types of fire but will not deal with smouldering fibrous materials. This is the best choice for a garage.

● Foam is suitable for flammable liquids but is usually too specialized for fires that occur in the home.

Trapped by fire

If you are trapped by fire gather the family together – in a front-facing room if possible. Remember that the landing may be too hot to cross and that smoke is as dangerous as flames. Follow these safety rules:

● **Close the door and block up the cracks with bedding.**

● **Go to the window and try to attract attention.**

● **Wait for the Fire brigade. If the room fills with smoke, put your head out of the window. If the smoke is outside too, get down on the floor, where the air is clearer.**

● **If you have to leave by the** window, don't jump – the fall may kill you. Make a rope out of bedding or throw a mattress or cushions out of the window first, to break your fall. Then let yourself down carefully, so that you are hanging by your fingertips from the window sill before you let go.

● **If you have to move through a smoke-filled house to escape, keep low. Test each door before opening it; if it is hot, don't open it.**

● **If your clothes catch fire, immediately roll on the ground to extinguish the flames or wrap yourself in a rug, blanket or towel.**

Fitting a smoke detector

Mains-operated detectors are far more complicated than battery operated models, which are fitted by screwing on the baseplate and then snapping on the cover. Battery-operated detectors are perfectly adequate, as long as you remember to change the batteries and test the system regularly.

The important considerations are which type to buy and where you are going to put it. Look for a potential escape route and place a detector with an integral safety light there.

Ceiling-mounted smoke detectors should be fitted at least 300mm(1ft) away from any wall or light fitting. Wall-mounted models should be 150-300mm(6-12in) below the ceiling. Remember that you'll need to service it, don't put it at the head of a stairwell or in any other inaccessible place. Temperature differences in the room can stop smoke reaching the detector, so don't put it on an uninsulated exterior wall or next to a heater or air conditioning vent. As always, look for the BS Kite marks when choosing a detector and, if in doubt, ask the local Fire brigade.

● Before fitting the detector, test it to make sure that it is working. Unclip the cover and connect the batteries, following the maker's instructions. Press the test button and wait for the alarm (about one minute on photoelectric models). The alarm will stop automatically after about ten seconds.

● For wall-mounted models, measure down about 150mm (6in) from the ceiling and offer up the baseplate. Mark the screw positions through the narrower end of the key-hole-shaped fixing holes and remove the baseplate.

● Drill and plug the wall and drive the screws halfway in. Position the baseplate on the screws and slide down to lock them into the narrow end of the keyhole slots.

● Tighten the screws. Beware of overtightening, or you may split the plastic casing.

● Snap in battery or batteries and press the cover on to the locating lugs in the baseplate.

● Test the apparatus again, using the test button.

● To position the detector on a ceiling, you'll need to locate a joist. Never fit it just on plasterboard or plaster. If necessary, span the gap between joists with a plank screwed into battens fixed to the joists.

● Offer up the baseplate as for wall fitting and mark the screw positions on the plaster with a bradawl. Then proceed as for a wall-mounted smoke detector.

● To link up two or more compatible detectors, run a thin bell wire between them to form a complete circuit. The most unobtrusive way to do this with ceiling-mounted fitments is to take the wire into the ceiling void. For wall-mounted models, work out the most unobtrusive route and clip or trunk the cable between each detector. It's best to have one upstairs and one downstairs.

● Make the connections within the detectors using purpose-built interconnecting devices with connector blocks. Strip, trim and twist about 12mm(½in) of the lead wires and screw this down under the terminals.

Fix detector 150mm(6in) below ceiling level

Check detector is firm and connect battery

Test the alarm and then replace the cover

FIRST AID

An understanding of simple First Aid techniques will give you the confidence to cope with most of the emergencies that you may encounter in or outside the home.

The following pages cover basic First Aid. But they are only a beginning: to be really proficient in First Aid techniques such as mouth-to-mouth resuscitation (kiss of life) and external chest compression, you should take a course run by one of the official First Aid bodies such as the St John Ambulance Brigade or the Red Cross. These widely available classes aim to teach all the basic life-saving techniques: resuscitation, how to control bleeding, how to deal with fractures, emergency child-birth, and so on – in short, what action to take in an emergency. Some of the courses have set examinations, and short-term certifications of proficiency are awarded.

If you took a First Aid course some time ago, you should consider repeating the classes as some First Aid techniques have changed over recent years.

Keeping yourself and others safe

On the following pages an alphabetical list of the most common accidents and injuries is given together with all the basic information you need to deal with them. However, certain emergency procedures have been deliberately omitted, as further injury can be caused to a casualty if treated by a well-meaning, but untrained person.

In any emergency act speedily but calmly. First assess the scene for possible danger, then take appropriate steps; for instance, cut off any gas supply, poisonous fumes, or electricity supply at source. If possible, send someone for help and a First Aid kit. If you are alone, quickly assess the casualty's condition and injuries so that you can decide whether to treat immediately or fetch a First Aid kit. In an unconscious casualty the priority is always to check for breathing. If there is no sign of breathing apply mouth-to-mouth resuscitation (see page 38). Try to keep calm and reassure the casualty in a soothing manner. If the injuries are serious or there is any doubt, call an ambulance as soon as possible.

Your home First Aid box

Although you can improvise dressings and bandages outside the home, every home should have its own First Aid box. Keep it in a handy place and make sure that used items are replaced. It should be airtight and contain:

cotton wool
sterile gauze

antiseptic lotion
medical disinfectant
a triangular bandage
assorted bandages
assorted prepared wound dressings
sterile eye pad with attachment
adhesive strip
safety pins
tweezers
blunt-ended scissors

Common accidents and how to treat them

BLEEDING – external

You should act quickly if large amounts of blood are being lost. Get medical help immediately and, in the meantime, try to stop the bleeding by applying pressure. If the wound is fairly small, apply fingertip pressure over the area; press very firmly over the wound and hold. If the wound is large and open, close it by pressing the edges of the cut together with thumbs. Maintain pressure for five to fifteen minutes. Lay the casualty down and raise the injured part, maintaining pressure on the wound. Cover the wound with a sterile, unmedicated dressing and tie firmly. If blood soaks through dressing, put another on top.

BURNS AND SCALDS

For minor household burns and scalds, cool the burn quickly by placing the injury under cold running water for at least ten minutes. Remove rings, watch or tight clothing before swelling occurs. Cover wound with a sterile gauze dressing: place gauze over burn and wind bandage around to cover. Secure firmly. Never put sticking plaster on a burn, and never put cotton wool or lint directly onto the wound as the fibres can become embedded.

If the person's clothing is on fire, put flames out by dousing with water or take a thick rug, jacket or towel, lay him on the floor and wrap the cloth firmly around to smother the flames. Press firmly but don't roll him around as this would expose other areas of the body to the flames. When the flames are out, remove burnt clothing but don't pull away anything that is stuck to the burnt area. Call an ambulance immediately.

CHOKING

If possible, treat the casualty in the position found. First remove any debris or false teeth from the mouth and encourage the casualty to cough. Help him to bend over with the head lower than the lungs. Using the heel of your hand, slap the casualty smartly between the shoulder blades up to four times; each slap should be hard enough to remove the obstruction. Check the mouth again. If the obstruction is visible but not coughed out, hook it out with your fingers.

For children follow just the same sequence, but either sit in a chair or kneel on one knee and lay the child over the other knee with the head down. Support the chest with one hand and slap the child smartly between the shoulder blades with the other.

ELECTRIC SHOCK

Separate the victim from the 'live' current as quickly as possible. Either switch off the main supply or use a non-conductive material such as a wooden broom handle or chair, and move the limb from the electrical appliance. Failing that, pull the victim away holding any loose clothing, but do not touch the flesh. Check for breathing and give mouth-to-mouth resuscitation if needed (see page 38). Place casualty in the recovery position (see right) and send for an ambulance immediately.

EPILEPSY

In a minor fit, first protect the person from any danger. Keep other people away, talk quietly to the casualty and then stay with him until fully recovered.

With a major attack, try to ease the fall and clear a space around the casualty. Loosen clothing around the neck and place something soft under the head. When convulsions cease, place casualty in recovery position (see right) and remain until he is fully recovered. Do not forcibly restrain the casualty or put anything in the mouth, and do not try to 'wake' the casualty.

FAINTING

If someone is feeling faint, sit him down and help him to lean forwards with the head between the knees, and to take deep breaths. **If the casualty is in a crowd** advise him to flex his toes and leg muscles to aid circulation. **If the person has fainted and is unconscious but breathing normally**, lay him down with legs raised and loosen any tight clothing at the neck, chest and waist. If, after a minute or two, the person has not gained consciousness, call medical aid. While the person is coming round, reassure him and gradually raise him to a sitting position. Do not give the casualty a drink unless fully conscious, and then only sips of water.

HEART ATTACK

The symptoms may vary from mild discomfort to extreme chest pain radiating down the left arm. The casualty may have a fast, weak or an irregular pulse, be pale, sweaty and may collapse. **Send for an ambulance immediately.** Mean-

Recovery position

An unconscious casualty who is breathing and whose heart is beating should be placed in the recovery position to keep the airway open and to drain any vomit or any other fluid from the mouth. Do not use the method shown here if the back or the lower body are injured, if the casualty is lying in a confined space, or if his limbs cannot be bent to support the body. In these situations place a firmly rolled blanket under one side of the casualty's body to support him in a simulated recovery position. Alternatively, keep the airway open (as in step 2 of mouth-to-mouth resuscitation). However, always use the recovery position if the casualty's breathing is difficult and noisy, or if you have to leave him alone.

1. With the casualty on his back, kneel at his right side (left if you are left-handed). Turn his head towards you and tilt it backwards slightly to open the airway

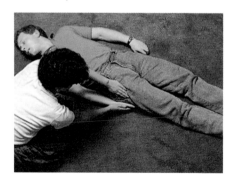

2. Place casualty's nearer arm straight by his side. Then place his palm upwards under his buttocks. Fold his other arm across his chest to touch his upper arm (as shown in step 3 photograph)

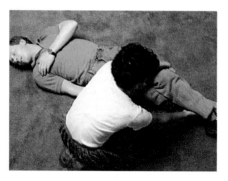

3. Cross casualty's further leg over his nearer leg at the ankle. Support the casualty's head with one hand. With the other hand, clasp the clothing at his hip and gently roll him towards you. Support him on your knees and turn him onto his front

4. Arrange the uppermost arm at right-angles to the casualty to support his upper body. Move the thigh of his uppermost leg upwards so that it is slightly bent. Gently pull his head back again to make sure that the airway is open

5. Pull the casualty's other arm out from underneath the body so that the forearm is parallel to his body. This will prevent the casualty from rolling over onto his back

while, place the casualty (if conscious) in a resting position with the upper body raised, and keep warm; cover with a blanket, jacket or coat. Loosen any tight clothing at neck and waist. If the patient becomes unconscious, mouth-to-mouth resuscitation together with external chest compression are required immediately. **This treatment should only be carried out by someone qualified to do so.**

INSECT STINGS

These are common in summer and mostly harmless. However, some people are allergic to the poison. **In case of allergy or multiple stings**, medical aid should be called immediately. The symptoms are sharp pain and swelling around the affected area with a reddish, central puncture mark. **If the sting is left in the skin**, try to remove it, preferably with tweezers held as near to the skin as possible. Do not squeeze the poison sac at the end of the sting as this will force in more poison. **To relieve pain and swelling**, apply a cold compress which has been soaked in surgical spirit. **For stings inside the mouth or throat**, give an ice cube (or ice lolly) to suck and take the casualty to hospital.

NOSEBLEED

Sit the person down with head well forward and loosen any tight clothing around the neck. Tell him to squeeze the soft part of his nose and breathe through the mouth, keeping his head down and maintaining pressure on the nose for ten minutes.

POISONING

Call an ambulance immediately in all cases. Never try to make the casualty vomit. **If a casualty vomits spontaneously**, clear nose and mouth to protect his breathing. **If he is unconscious and breathing becomes difficult**, put the casualty in the recovery position (see page 37). Try to establish which poison and how much has been swallowed or inhaled and let the doctor know. Give him or her a sample of the poison and its container, if possible.

Mouth-to-mouth resuscitation

If you find a person unconscious, check quickly for injuries and control any bleeding. If it is safe to do so, turn the casualty on to his back. To prevent the tongue blocking the windpipe, tilt the head right back so that the tongue moves upwards with the jaw.

If the casualty is breathing, and it is safe to do so, turn him into the recovery position (see page 37).

If the casualty is not breathing, begin immediate resuscitation. Use mouth-to-mouth resuscitation (the 'kiss of life') in most cases, as below. Do not use this method when the casualty has severe facial injuries, is vomiting frequently, has poison around the mouth, or is pinned face down. If necessary, ventilation can be performed through the casualty's nose. Other resuscitation methods are taught at first aid classes.

If you find a person unknown to you unconscious, always check their body, clothing and belongings for any medical card, bracelet or necklace giving details of epilepsy, diabetes or other condition. It's most important to give anything you find to the ambulance crew.

1. Place the casualty on his back and bend down over his mouth to listen for breathing. Look along the casualty's chest and abdomen to check for any sign of breathing.

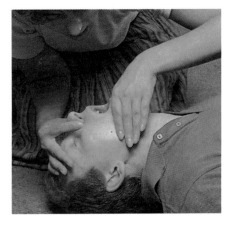

3. Open casualty's mouth by placing one hand on chin. Place other hand over his forehead, at the same time pinching nose closed. Take a deep breath and blow in

2. Remove any obstructions from face or neck and open the casualty's airway: with one hand under neck and other on forehead, tilt head right back. Remove any debris from mouth or throat with your fingers

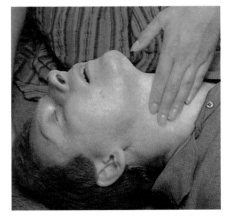

4. Remove mouth and breathe out excess air. Repeat step 3. Continue until the casualty is breathing. If casualty is not breathing, check that the airway is clear (see step 2). If necessary, treat for choking

HOME STYLE

The key to successful decorating lies in good planning and careful preparation; get that right, and any job you tackle will go smoothly.

Decorating is by far the most popular do-it-yourself activity, for several reasons. It's not difficult – you can get good results even if you aren't an expert, which you can't with things like plastering or bricklaying – and it's very rewarding to see the fruits of your labours in the form of a newly-decorated room. Above all, it saves you so much money, because the materials are comparatively cheap and you don't pay for your own labour.

Before taking you through what's involved in three of the most popular decorating projects – painting your house, papering a room and tiling a bathroom – here is some background information that will help you to get ready for redecorating.

Preparing woodwork

Most people paint their interior woodwork, although there is currently a trend towards more use of natural wood finishes such as stains and varnishes. If yours is painted, your first step should always be to wash it down thoroughly with sugar soap or strong detergent, to remove surface dirt and grease. As you do this, look out for any areas that are chipped or flaking; they will need touching in with primer and undercoat (and filler too if the wood is damaged) before repainting begins. Then go over all the surfaces with fine wet-and-dry abrasive paper, used wet, to remove any specks of dust caught in the paint last time you decorated. This process also 'flattens' the existing gloss surface

and improves the adhesion of the new paint. Wipe down the surfaces with clean water and leave them to dry.

If you are using a similar colour to what's there, one fresh coat of paint is usually all that's needed. But if you are changing to a completely different colour scheme, it's best to use an undercoat first followed by one top coat, rather than to use two coats of gloss.

Remember that on less-than-perfect paintwork, an eggshell paint with a silk or satin finish will help disguise the surface imperfections; high gloss finishes just highlight them.

You may decide you're tired of paint, and would like to give some or all of your woodwork a natural finish instead. This means stripping off all the old paint – a tedious and time-consuming process involving using a hot air gun (or a blowlamp if you prefer the traditional tool), plus paint stripper for bits the gun won't reach. You can save a lot of time – and effort – by sending doors to be professionally stripped while you tackle the fixed woodwork.

If your woodwork already has a natural finish, it may need nothing more than a wash down to restore it. However, if the finish has dulled, just apply a fresh coat of clear varnish – gloss or satin.

Preparing walls and ceilings

If your walls and ceilings are painted and you simply want a change of colour, all you need to do is to wash down the surfaces as for woodwork, rinse them off and leave them to dry. Seal nicotine and water stains by overpainting them with a solvent-based paint, or else use a special aerosol sealer. Then put on a fresh coat of emulsion paint.

If you want to hang wallpaper, you can go right ahead if your walls are painted plaster; simply size the surfaces first with diluted wallpaper paste to improve the new wallpaper's slip during hanging and its adhesion afterwards. But if the surfaces are already papered, the old paper must come off. With vinyls, peel off the plastic top layer dry, then soak and scrape off the absorbent backing paper. With washables and painted wallpapers, it's best to hire a steam stripper; stripping by hand is very time-consuming.

Tackling textured finishes

Textured finishes are particularly popular for ceilings, but can be used on walls too. All they need to freshen them up is a new coat of emulsion paint, but if you want to replace them with a different finish, life becomes a little more difficult. What you do depends on what you've got, since there are two main types of textured finish.

The first is what everyone calls Artex, although this is just one of several brands. The best way of removing this is to use a steam stripper, which softens the compound and allows you to scrape it off – a messy job, but it does work.

The second type is a textured emulsion paint, and to remove this you need to use special textured paint remover. This works like any other paint stripper, making the paint bubble and blister so you can scrape it off. However, you need to take great care when using it, especially on ceilings. Wear safety goggles, gloves and some sort of protective headgear to guard against splashes on your skin, and put down plenty of dustsheets to protect furniture and floorcoverings.

HOUSE PAINTING

**Decorating the outside of your home
doesn't just give it a bright, clean, new
look: painting walls, windows and
doors also provides essential
protection against the elements. Arm
yourself with the right equipment and
adopt a strict strategy to produce a
smart appearance that will last,
whatever the weather, for years.**

Exposed to the seasonal rigours of rain,
wind, snow and sun, houses can soon
become shabby. If left for too long, your
house will need more than just a coat of
paint, as flaky, blistered paintwork will
admit moisture to the underlying surface. This will cause, amongst other
problems, rot in timber, rust in metalwork, or damp in walls, all of which
need considerable attention to put right.

So applying a new lick of paint is an
essential part of an overall maintenance
plan, which must be carried out regularly. And it's essential that you prepare
the surfaces properly first, otherwise
the finish will deteriorate quickly and
you'll have to do it over again.

What the job involves

Painting the outside of your house calls
for a strict plan of action.
● Make good defects in surfaces – fill
cracks and holes in masonry, patch or
replace rotten timber, remove rust from
metal, repair faulty guttering.
● Clean sound surfaces by washing
down with detergent to remove grime,

treat algae or growths of mould, or
brush to remove dust and flaky paint.
● Strip off unsound, previous paint
finishes (wood and metal) or key sound
finishes for repainting.
● Prime bare timber and metal or
porous masonry with primer.
● Apply paint system of undercoat and
top coats (wood and metal) and the
required number of coats of wall paint.

BEFORE YOU START . . .
● Inspect the house thoroughly and
decide which repairs need to be made
prior to painting. Check whether the
guttering is sound and remember to
examine the flashings which seal the
join between the roof and the walls, or

between the chimney and the roof.

● Choose the colours and types of paint you want to use, bearing in mind the various surfaces.

● Collect all the tools and equipment you will need for the preparation work (see Checklist on page 40).

● Decide on what decorating tools you're going to use. For woodwork and metalwork brushes are best. You'll need a selection of sizes: a 25mm (1in) angled-bristle cutting-in brush for glazing bars; 50mm (2in) for frames and mouldings; and 75mm (3in) for larger areas. For walls you have the choice between brushes, rollers and spray equipment. Brushes are always a good choice, but the largest size you'll need – 100mm (4in) at least – can be heavy and tiring to use for long periods. Rollers – choose a long-pile variety, not the foam type – enable you to apply the paint quickly but aren't ideal for textured walls. Spray guns – which can be hired – offer the quickest method of application but you have to mask off all areas you don't want to paint.

● Arrange suitable access. If you're just painting gutters and window frames on the first floor you can probably manage from an extending ladder, but if you're tackling the walls, too, a platform tower provides safer access. Aluminium or wooden layers and slot-together alloy towers can be hired.

WATCH OUT FOR . . .

Weather problems. Start decorating in late spring or early summer, when the timber and masonry surfaces have had the chance to dry out. Begin on a warm, dry day (there shouldn't have been rain, fog or frost for at least 24 hours). Don't paint in full sun, as the paint will dry out too rapidly, causing blistering and cracking: follow the sun around, so newly painted surfaces can dry slowly.

● Painting over a defective surface. Unless surfaces are thoroughly prepared any subsequent paint finish you apply will fail.

● Starting a job you can't finish in one session. If you can paint only half a wall before having to break off you'll find a hard edge will be visible when you restart. Aim to paint up to a corner or other feature dividing a wall.

Prepare the walls

The walls are the first parts to tackle. Potentially the most messy, they're also the largest areas.

Arrange access equipment – ladders or a platform tower – then, working from the top of the wall downwards, start your preparation.

If the wall structure is sound but grubby, use a stiff-bristled hand brush to remove dust. Don't use a wire brush; it scratches the surface and deposits strands which rust and mar the finish. Scrub and hose down grimy patches, but if you use a detergent, make sure that you rinse it off thoroughly before you start the painting.

TIP . . .

Algae or mould growths – caused by dampness in walls – are likely to reappear on your new finish unless you eradicate the spores. Cure the damp problem (say a leaky pipe or faulty DPC) then apply a strong bleach solution or proprietary fungicide. Leave for 24 hours,

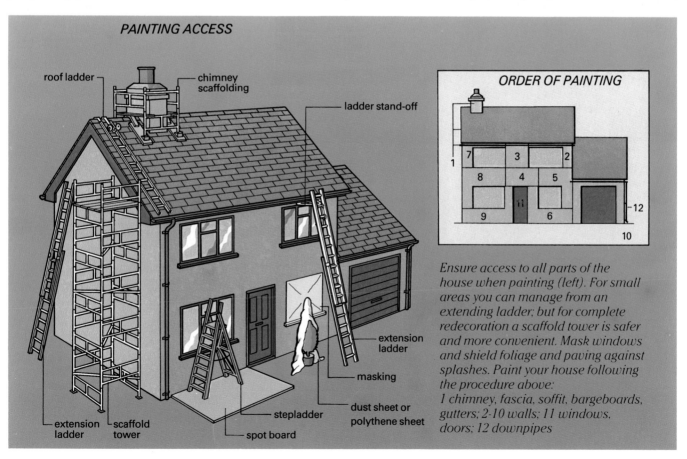

PAINTING ACCESS

roof ladder — chimney scaffolding

ladder stand-off

extension ladder

masking

dust sheet or polythene sheet

stepladder

spot board

extension ladder — scaffold tower

ORDER OF PAINTING

1 7 3 2
8 4 5
11
9 6
10
12

Ensure access to all parts of the house when painting (left). For small areas you can manage from an extending ladder; but for complete redecoration a scaffold tower is safer and more convenient. Mask windows and shield foliage and paving against splashes. Paint your house following the procedure above:
1 chimney, fascia, soffit, bargeboards, gutters; 2-10 walls; 11 windows, doors; 12 downpipes

scrub the treated area then rinse well with clean water. Repeat if necessary.

Powdery, chalky old finishes don't make a good base for new paint, so brush them down then apply a stabilizing solution or masonry sealer, using a large brush. The liquid is colourless and can be overpainted.

Old coats of paint which are beginning to flake must be removed prior to repainting. Use a wide-bladed metal scraper to remove loose material. Smooth with abrasive paper then wash to remove dust.

Bare brick walls can be painted for a bright finish or to conceal previous repairs, but if the faces are spalling – separating due to frost attack – or if the mortar pointing is crumbly or loose, repair the damage first. You will have to patch and render badly spalled bricks: repair isn't possible.

Rake out defective pointing with a cold chisel and repoint with fresh mortar, or pointing compound (sold in cartridge form and ideal for small areas). Fill any minor cracks in the brick-work with an external filler, then sand down the repairs.

Cracks in render less than about 2mm (1/16in) wide will be filled with the paint alone, but wider defects must be made good with exterior-grade filler. Rake out loose material and widen the edges – undercutting so the filler will grip – using a cold chisel and club hammer. Flick out dust with an old paintbrush then dampen the crack so that the filler

2. Use a scraper to remove old flaking paint for masonry. For powdery surfaces use a brush

3. Treat patches of algae or mould with a strong bleach solution or proprietary fungicide

won't dry out too quickly and crack. Spread filler along the crack with a flexible-bladed knife, forcing it well in. When the filler has set, smooth with abrasive paper flush with the rendering.

Check for areas of blown render, where the render has separated from the masonry. Tapping lightly with a hammer reveals hollow parts. If you find any, hack off the unsound render and undercut it to sound edges. Dampen the exposed masonry then trowel on fresh cement render to fill the hole. Apply two coats of render for deep holes, allowing the first to set completely before beginning to apply the second.

TIP . . .

Pebbledashing isn't usually painted, but if blown areas have been heavily patched the pebbles and mortar used will probably not match the rest of the wall and a coat of paint will conceal the repairs and help loose pebbles to stick.

Cleaning up

● If splashes do occur, then choose the appropriate solvent for that type of paint: for emulsions that means plenty of clean water; for oil-based paints, such as gloss or most varnishes, use white spirit.

● Do not let paint splashes dry. Scoop off paint, then sponge the area with the correct solvent.

● If the paint has been allowed to dry, first try treating it as if it were wet paint. If that does not work, moisten emulsion splashes with a little methylated spirit, which will soften the paint and allow the water to get in. Failing that, try a brush-cleaning fluid.

● Keep a cloth moistened with white spirit or dampened with water, handy beside you, to mop up spills immediately.

● Use a 'solid' emulsion or a non-drip paint if you are a messy painter.

● Brushes that have been used for emulsion should be cleaned under a cold water tap as soon as you have finished using them. Brushes that have been used for oil-based paints need to be soaked in white spirit.

1. Starting at the top, wash down dirty walls with a stiff scrubbing brush and soapy water, then rinse off the detergent very thoroughly

4. Patch badly damaged or spalled brickwork and renew pointing if it is necessary, then paint or render to conceal the repairs

Prepare wood and metal

1. Treat rotten frames with wood hardener, then fill and insert preservative pellets

2. Remove thick paint layers on windows and doors with a chemical paint stripper

With the walls prepared, tackle the doors, windows, fascias, soffits and bargeboards – and prepare gutters and downpipes for repainting.

In the case of **wooden windows and doors**, replace seriously rotten timber by cutting-in new wood, or treat salvageable parts with a proprietary three-part wood repair system, comprising wood hardener high-performance filler and preservative pellets to ward against future outbreaks of rot. Fill small cracks and dents with flexible wood filler.

If glazing putty is crumbly or loose chop it out using an old chisel and clean up the rebate. It is important to prime the surface after having cleaned it, or the new material will not stick. Then press in new linseed oil or all-purpose putty and form neat bevels (putty must be left for about ten days prior to painting).

Sand sound, previously painted woodwork to key the glossy finish to accept the new coat of paint. Wash it down using mild detergent to remove grease and grime, then rinse the area with plenty of clean water and allow it to dry completely.

Old paintwork which is chipped, blistered or otherwise defective must be made good. If the defects are localized, scrape the paint away until you reach firm edges, sand the area smooth then rinse it with white spirit before spot-priming with wood primer. Where defects are widespread, strip off the entire finish to bare wood, using a hot air gun or blowtorch.

TIP . . .
Use chemical paint stripper around the edges of window panes and glazed door panels so there's no risk of shattering the glass with the heat from a hot air gun or blowtorch.

Treat painted timber cladding as for other joinery or, if it's previously been varnished, remove the finish with a chemical varnish stripper then prime before painting.

Hardwood doors, subframes and window sills are generally varnished or treated with a stain and preservative suited for outdoor use, so it's best not to paint them.

Metal window and door frames – not the modern aluminium but the older steel types – are susceptible to rusting if moisture penetrates the paint film. Rub down minor rust spots with wire wool or abrasive paper but scrape off any flaky paint and rust with a wire brush, then rub smooth with abrasive paper.

Cast iron gutters and downpipes should be wire-brushed to remove flaky paint and rust, then smoothed with abrasive paper. Minor cracks and leaky joints can be patched with cartridge-applied mastic.

Paint highest parts

Start by painting the highest areas of the house – fascias, soffits, bargeboards and gutters. If you leave them until after you've painted the walls there is always the risk that you may splash paint down on to the freshly-decorated walls, spoiling the general effect.

Apply a coat of matt undercoat to the soffit, bargeboards and fascias, which cover the ends of the roof rafters. Use a medium-size brush, applying the paint along the grain. Allow to dry (this takes about 12 hours) before sanding lightly with fine glasspaper. Dust off using a tacky rag (sold in DIY stores), then apply a coat of gloss. When the gloss is completely dry, sand lightly, dust off and apply a second coat.

TIP . . .
Because soffits, fascias and bargeboards are so exposed to the elements, they deteriorate much quicker than other areas of exterior woodwork. For extra protection, apply a third coat of gloss, after sanding and dusting off.

Now is the time to paint the gutters (not the downpipes). Treat bare metal with red lead or zinc chromate primer, then apply undercoat and top coats. If gutters have been previously painted with bituminous paint, use this for the new coat. However, black is the standard colour for bituminous paint (there

Apply the correct undercoat to the woodwork, then sand lightly and dust off with a tacky rag before applying a top-coat of gloss.

1. Paint soffits, fascias and bargeboards with an extra coat of gloss for added protection

2. Mix leftover paint and use it to paint the inside of the gutters where it doesn't show

are other colours but the choice is extremely limited).

If you want to use ordinary gloss you must apply an aluminium sealer first, so the bitumen won't bleed through and spoil the finish. Alternatively, use a modified bituminous paint, which contains aluminium to prevent bleeding.

TIP . . .
Use up leftover gloss paint, mixed together, for the insides of gutters. Colour is immaterial, as it won't be visible from ground level. Strain the blended paint – through a pair of nylon tights – before use.

Paint the walls

The walls are the second – and largest – area to paint and should be divided into sections you can tackle in one session.

Try to split the walls into sections using downpipes, window bays, corners and other features as divisions, so hard edges won't be visible should you have to break off before completing the job. Always start painting from the top right-hand corner of a wall, working down and across.

If you're using a brush, apply the paint in bold criss-cross strokes; move onto the next section and blend in the wet edges.

TIP . . .
On heavily textured walls you'll find it easier to use a stiff-bristled banister brush with a stippling action to force the paint into the rough surface.

If you're using a roller for the walls, you still have to use a brush to paint around the perimeter of each bay, since the roller can't reach into corners and edges. Adopt the same criss-cross application when using the brush.

TIP . . .
Rollers usually come with a hollow-ended handle into which you can fit an ordinary broomstick, for reaching otherwise inaccessible parts of the wall.

1. Cover nearby plants and bushes, and mask windows and doors before applying paint with a spray

If you want to use a pressurized spray gun to paint the walls, first mask off with newspaper or polythene all parts you don't want to paint, sticking it down with masking tape. Cover paving and foliage below the area being painted to protect them from splashes (paint on paving is hard to remove).

Apply the paint in overlapping horizontal bands, working from the top right-hand corner towards a natural break. To avoid runs, keep the gun constantly on the move. When you've sprayed the wall, remove the masking and carefully touch in areas around doors, windows and other features with a brush.

Apply subsequent coats of primer to the walls before painting the joinery.

2. Paint heavily textured wall finishes with a stiff-bristle banister brush to give even coverage

3. Fit a broomstick onto a paint roller handle to reach less accessible sections of wall

Paint windows and doors

Timber or metal windows and doors are painted after the walls. The first job is to prime bare areas.

On softwood frames and doors, use a wood or acrylic primer, or an aluminium wood primer for resinous wood. Red lead or zinc chromate primers are used for iron and steel.

When the primer has dried, apply the relevant undercoat that's compatible with the gloss of your choice. Rub down the undercoat lightly when it's dry, then brush on a coat of gloss. Work along the wood grain, finishing with light laying-off strokes to avoid brush marks. When the first coat has dried, sand lightly, dust off and apply a second coat. On exposed elevations, apply a third coat.

TIP . . .

Water-based microporous gloss paints, which dry to a film featuring tiny pores to let the wood breathe, need to be applied straight on to bare wood without undercoat. If you apply microporous paint to a surface that is simply keyed for a top coat, the original coating will seal and "suffocate" the wood and the microporous properties of the top coat will be lost.

Use an angle-bristled cutting-in brush for painting glazing bars or, if you don't trust the steadiness of your hand, stick masking tape on the glass to give a neat line. Peel off the tape when the paint is touch-dry, or you could lift this off too. Alternatively, buy a plastic paint shield, which you hold against the glass to guide the brush. Nevertheless, carry the paint about 3mm (⅛in) onto the glass to prevent moisture seeping beneath.

Paint windows and doors in sequence for a neat, even finish.

To paint a door, wedge it open with a wooden block, then remove the door furniture. Slip newspaper or plastic sheeting under the door to protect the floor from drips. Apply primer, undercoat and gloss in the usual paint system.

TIP . . .

Remember to brush from the edges, not onto them, to avoid a build-up of paint,

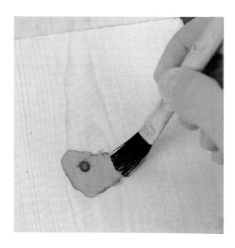

1. Treat knots on new windows and doors with shellac knotting before applying a coat of primer

2. Use a plastic paint shield to protect the glass when painting windows and doors

which could cause a door or window to bind in its frame. Don't be tempted to close a door or window before you are sure it is dry.

Paint a flush door in this sequence: start with the frame, then tackle the top, bottom and side edges and finally paint the face.

Paint a panelled door in this sequence: the panels and mouldings; the vertical rails; the horizontal rails and the outer stiles. Paint the hinge edge the same colour as the outside face.

Paint the downpipes

The rainwater system's downpipes are the very last item you should paint, starting as always from the top and working your way down.

Hold a piece of cardboard or plastic behind each section of the downpipe as you paint to protect the newly-painted wall from splashes or smears (difficult to remove when dry). Apply the paint in vertical strokes, not horizontal ones, which will certainly splatter paint at each side. Finish each section with light downward strokes so brush marks won't show.

Before starting to paint plastic pipes, they should be rubbed down lightly with abrasive paper to key the surface.

1. Paint the downpipe using a piece of cardboard to shield the masonry from accidental splashes

2. Finish the downpipe with two coats of gloss. Plastic pipes can be keyed, then painted as usual

PAPERING A ROOM

When it comes to decorating a room, wallpaper remains a firm favourite. It's a quick and effective way to give colour, pattern – and even texture – to a large surface. Master the skills and you will be able to apply them to any room in your house.

Invariably, the most difficult aspect of wallpapering a room is choosing the paper. Putting it up is easy – once you know the ropes – and can even be enjoyable. To begin with, select the most appropriate type of covering – such as a relief paper to disguise uneven surfaces or an easy-clean vinyl for children's rooms or steamy rooms.

Colour and pattern are equally important considerations and can have a dramatic effect on your decor. Remember that light, pale colours 'create' space while dark shades and bold designs tend to make a room appear much smaller. Use soft, warm tones and colours – conducive to relaxation – in living-rooms and bedrooms and keep stimulating, primary colours for kitchens, playrooms and workrooms.

What the job involves

When papering a room, it is quite easy to achieve a professional finish. But it is just as easy to make mistakes that remain glaringly obvious – until you redecorate. For good-looking results, approach the job methodically and give plenty of time to initial preparations.
● Measure the room's walls and, if applicable, ceiling.
● Use these dimensions to estimate how many rolls of paper are needed; allow extra for patterns.
● Buy the materials. Choose the correct type of paste as recommended by the paper manufacturer.
● Clean and prepare all surfaces to be papered: strip off old paper, flaking paint and distemper; fill cracks and make good other defects.
● Seal dusty and porous surfaces, especially new plaster, with size.
● If woodwork – doors, windows, skirtings – is to be repainted, do this before papering.
● Mix up the wallpaper paste.

● Cut lengths of paper to slightly over size – allow more for patterned types so you can match one strip with another. Spread with a suitable wallpaper paste.
● Hang the lengths, smooth down and trim to fit.
● Wipe off excess paste from paper and adjacent paintwork.

BEFORE YOU START . . .
● Make sure you have enough paper for the job. If you underestimate your needs and have to buy extra rolls later, there may be problems with colour matching. Most suppliers will take back un-used rolls provided they are un-opened and in good condition.
● Choose the correct paste (available

in powder form or ready-mixed) for the paper being hung. Paste comes in three grades: ordinary for conventional wallpaper; heavy-duty for heavier papers and embossed coverings; fungicidal paste – to prevent mould growth – for washables, vinyls, metallized foils and foamed polyethylene (Novamura).
● Prepare old surfaces thoroughly.
● Existing wallcoverings must be stripped: score the surface with a wire brush or toothed scraper, then soak with a solution of warm water and washing-up liquid or use a proprietary stripper. For large areas, consider hiring a steam stripper. Painted surfaces must be washed with detergent, then keyed with a wire brush or coarse-grade glasspaper. Fill cracks and small holes.

Checklist

Tools
tape measure
pencil
scissors (large)
bucket
pasting table
paste brush
plumb line (chalked)
hanging brush
sponge
seam roller
trimming knife
step-ladder

Materials
wallpaper
paste
size (optional)

● Treat new plasterboard with a primer-sealer. Coat bare plaster – new and old – with size. Use either a commercial size or a weak solution of wallpaper paste. Once a wall is sealed with size, it absorbs paste more slowly so giving you more time to position lengths of wall-paper correctly.

● On uneven surfaces and for an expert finish – particularly with heavy-weight papers – line walls before papering. Lining paper, hung horizontally, provides a fine, even base for the final covering. It also helps to disguise any surface imperfections and provides an insulating layer quite cheaply.

● Remove as much furniture as possible – stack the rest in the middle of the room, roll up carpets and cover everything with dustsheets.

● Check that you can reach all areas easily. Generally a platform step-ladder is adequate for papering walls, but for ceilings use a scaffold board between two step-ladders or other suitably sturdy supports.

● Allow enough time to complete the job in daylight. By artificial light, bubbles are hard to spot.

● Decide where to begin papering. In general, start alongside a window or

Paper the room in a logical order, either from a focal point and work out, or from a window or door

door. But if the room has a dominant feature – like a chimney breast – begin there, especially with a bold-patterned paper; hang one strip centrally and work outwards from either side.

WATCH OUT FOR . . .

● Batch numbers. Wallcoverings are printed in batches: rolls from the same batch have good colour matching, but there may be some variation between different batches. Check that all the rolls you have bought actually do have the same batch number.

● Pattern. Wallcoverings have various types of pattern. Some patterns are random and no matching between lengths is required; some line up horizontally. Others, termed drop patterns, run diagonally; buy extra paper for matching these: one or two rolls according to the pattern repeat size.

● Shade variations. Even within the same batch, slight differences in colour can occur. If the variation is obvious, minimize it by putting matching rolls on the same wall.

● New plaster. Allow new plaster to dry out thoroughly, for at least six months, before papering.

● Fungicide in paste and size. Keep preparations away from children and pets; wash hands after use.

● Problem papers. Ordinary wallpaper is not very strong and readily tears, especially when wet with paste. Flock papers stain easily: so it is important to wipe off splashes immediately.

Fold-up pasting tables can be bought or hired. Alternatively, use a table or board at least 1.8m(6ft) long

Estimating

An accurate estimate of quantities is essential – if you do not buy enough rolls to begin with you may have matching problems later. Working out how much you need is quite easy as most papers come in standard-size rolls: 10.05m(33ft) long and 530mm(21in) wide. Some coverings, however – particularly special finishes and imports – can vary in width or length.

To help you work out quantities, most retailers have tables showing the number of rolls needed in relation to area. Before consulting these tables, you must know the height of your room and the distance round the walls: include

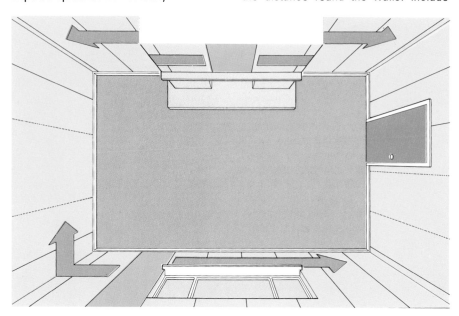

doors, windows and built-in cupboards unless they are very large.

You can also estimate how many rolls you need by counting out the room in strips of wallpaper. Start by measuring the height of the wall from skirting to ceiling; add on 100mm(4in) for trimming and, with a drop pattern, half the distance of the repeat. Divide this length into the total roll length to give the number of strips you get from one roll.

Now cut a piece of string to the width of the roll. From one corner, go round the room counting the number of widths needed to cover all walls. Divide this number by the number of strips you can get from one roll to calculate the number of rolls required.

The same principle can be applied to ceiling estimates.

When estimating paper quantities, use a length of string to represent the width of a roll

Cutting and pasting

Measure the wall height and add on 50mm(2in) at each end for trimming and easing. Cut the first drop from the roll using scissors or by tearing it against a straightedge. Lay the drop face up on the pasting table and use it as a guide for matching and cutting the next drop. Continue in this way, cutting all the full lengths needed to cover the room; number each drop as you cut it. Leave awkward areas until you come to them.

TIP . . .
If possible, stand the pasting table in front of a window and face the window

when pasting. The daylight will then show up any unpasted areas. Lengths should be completely covered with adhesive to avoid air bubbles and parting seams when dry.

Stack the drops in numerical order, face down with the first one on top. Allow the top edges of the lengths to overhang the far end of the table by about 20mm(¾in); the other ends should hang on the floor. Line up the side edges with the furthest edge of the table, letting it overhang slightly so that the table top stays free of paste.

Mix up the paste and leave it to stand for 15 minutes – or according to the manufacturer's instructions – and then give a final stir to ensure there are no lumps. Stretch a string across the top of the paste bucket to provide something to wipe the brush against.

1. Start by pasting a strip down the centre then work outwards to each edge in a zig-zag pattern

2. Fold the ends to the middle and leave to soak then carry the paper over your arm

Apply the paste, brushing it outwards in zig-zag pattern from the centre to the far edge. Then slide the paper towards you so that the unpasted section overhangs the near side of the table. Coat this with paste in the same way.

When all the paper area on the table is pasted, fold the length over, paste to paste. Slide the rest of the drop on to the table for pasting and then fold to the middle in the same way so that you can carry it into place and hang it.

Set the pasted length aside to soak (see manufacturer's instructions) while you paste subsequent drops. Paste about three lengths of medium weight paper at a time so the first is ready to hang by the time you've pasted the third. Mark the top of each length with pencil so you hang it the right way up.

TIP . . .
If you are unsure which way up a pattern goes, note that the top of the pattern is always at the beginning of a roll as you open it. When cutting bold-patterned paper, arrange it so that a complete motif appears at the top of the wall – it looks better there than half way down.

Hanging and trimming

Use the plumb line (see *tip* on page 49) to mark a vertical on the wall at your starting point. Take the first pasted sheet, unfold the top half and position it against the wall. Place the paper so that about 50mm(2in) overlaps on to the ceiling and the edge aligns with your guide line. Slide the paper gently by pressing your palms flat against it.

With a hanging brush (or a soft cloth) smooth the paper into the ceiling angle. Then work down the middle, brushing towards the sides to remove all pockets of air.

After finishing the top half, unfold the bottom section of the drop and repeat the process. At the base, brush the paper firmly into the skirting. If you find the paper is going up crooked, simply peel off and start again from the top.

To trim, run the back of your scissors along the ceiling angle to make a crease. Carefully pull the paper away, cut along the crease line, then brush the paper back flat. Repeat at the skirting. When trimming, scissors are less likely to tear paper than a knife.

Hang the second drop in the same way, carefully sliding it into place so that the pattern lines up and the edges of the lengths butt together tightly. In general, avoid overlapping drops.

At corners, measure the distance between the edge of the last drop hung and the corner at top, middle and bottom. Few corners are truly vertical, and the paper will form bubbles if you simply paste it around both walls of a corner. Take the longest measurement and add 13mm(½in) to it. Cut a strip from the next pasted sheet to this width, then hang the sheet so that the excess turns on to the adjacent wall. If the wall is very uneven you may need to slit the overlapping section to prevent creases.

Measure the width of the offcut and mark the new vertical guideline on the unpapered wall this distance from the corner. Hang the offcut to this line; any mismatch of pattern will go unnoticed.

TIP . . .

Make a small cut at top and bottom corners so that you can smooth both faces against the wall surface without difficulty. Trim to length.

At light and socket fittings, turn off the electricity supply. Smooth the paper lightly over the fitting and make four cuts in the shape of a star. Trim off the waste, leaving a slight margin. Remove the faceplate, brush the paper flat underneath and replace the plate.

Sponge off any excess paste from skirting and ceiling before it dries.

TIP . . .

Make your own plumb line by tying a small heavy object, like a bolt, to a length of fine string. Tape the end of the string to the wall and let the weight hang free until it stops swinging.

To mark the vertical on the wall, either draw along the plumb line with a pencil or rub a piece of chalk along the string before use. When the vertical has been established, hold the bottom of the string taut and twang it against the wall. It will leave a mark which can be used as a guide for positioning the paper.

1. Hold the plumb line taut and snap its chalked string against the wall to give a true vertical.

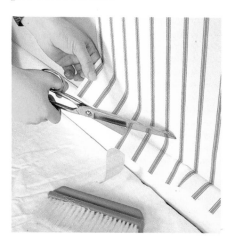

2. At ceiling and skirting levels, crease the paper into the join and use it as a guide for trimming

3. Use a seam roller to flatten down joins. On embossed coverings smooth the seams with a clean, soft brush

4. At corners cut the paper so that about 13mm(½in) curves round, then hang the rest on the adjacent wall

5. Trim off excess paper round electrical fittings, switch power off then tuck edges under

Ceilings

Surprisingly, ceilings – generally obstacle-free except for a light fitting – are as easy to paper as walls. But it is essential to have suitable access equipment so that you can work at a safe, comfortable height.

It is simplest to work across the narrowest width of the room, starting at the window end. The paper should be cut and pasted in the same way as for walls but fold the lengths, paste to paste, concertina fashion; make each fold about 300mm(12in) long.

To position the first length, make a guideline on the ceiling: measure out from the wall the full width of the covering less a 13mm(½in) margin.

Carry the paper more easily by draping it over a spare roll or cardboard tube: then use the roll to support the folded portion while you brush the first section into place. As on walls, smooth the paper into the angles, crease it and trim off the excess. If the walls are also to be papered, then allow the ceiling paper to overlap by 13mm(½in). Make V-cuts in the overlap to fit round chimney breast corners, etc. Roll all seams flat and sponge off any surplus paste.

Deal with ceiling roses in the same manner as wall switches and sockets. Always remember to turn off the electricity at the mains before taking down electrical fittings and loosening the covers of roses.

Fold ceiling paper concertina-fashion and support it with a batten while brushing the paper flat

Awkward areas

All rooms have awkward features – if only a door and window. But papering round them is not a problem – just keep the following points in mind.

Doors. Brush the paper down to the top of the door frame, crease it and make a horizontal cut. Then smooth the paper tight against the frame. Mark and trim off excess at the sides as you would at the top or bottom of a drop. If you are left with a very narrow strip of paper down one side of the door, consider hanging a narrow piece centrally above the door. This will push the next drop further along and so make the border next to the frame wider.

Mantelshelves. Treat these in the same way as doors, but watch out for intricate trims round mouldings.

TIP . . .

When papering stairwells, the major problem is handling the long length. Make sure you have adequate access equipment as well as an assistant – to take the weight of the drop while you position it.

Windows. Brush the first drop down from the ceiling and make two horizontal cuts – at window top and bottom – so that a portion can be turned in onto the side of the reveal. Paste the rest of the drop to the wall below the window. Continue across the top and bottom with

1. Fold paper into a reveal and fill in gaps with offcuts positioned under the main drops

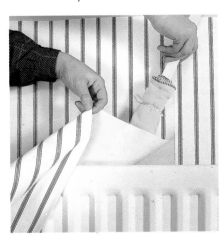

2. Gently push strips of paper down behind a radiator using a thin batten covered with a cloth

more drops, turning the upper sections on to the top of the reveal and trimming them at the window frame edges.

At the other end of the window opening, hang another complete drop, turning a portion on to the side of the reveal. Cut small patches to fill in any gaps on the reveal; on the top side of the reveal, feed these patches under the paper on the face of the wall by about 13mm(½in).

Pipes. Paste the paper and hang it over the pipe. Smooth down lightly and cut the covering up the middle over the pipe. Ease the two sections so they fit neatly behind the pipe and smooth down with a brush.

TIP . . .

Keep offcuts as they may be useful for repairing damage or papering awkward places – such as the top of a reveal.

Radiators. Mark the position of the brackets on the radiator, then hang the length of paper on the wall above. Cut long, vertical slits in the paper to correspond with the bracket marking. If the brackets are very wide cut out a wider section of paper to fit round them. Push the strips down behind the radiator. Butt-join the strips at the base of the radiator and trim lengths along skirting boards.

Correcting faults

If you find that there is a crease in the paper after hanging, it has happened either because the walls are out of true or because you have not brushed down the walls properly. Correct the fault by gently peeling the paper away from the wall to a point above the crease. Brush the paper back towards the adjacent drop first, then brush it towards the free side and finally brush the paper downwards.

If wallpaper is not pasted properly, or is not allowed to soak for long enough, air bubbles may appear. To flatten a bubble, puncture it with a tip of a blade or a craft knife, press out the air inside, then smooth the paper flat.

TILING A BATHROOM

Ceramic tiles are ideal for bathrooms because they'll resist soap, water and steam. They are surprisingly easy to fix and even awkward shapes and difficult access areas can be tackled if you take care and have patience.

A half or fully tiled bathroom will protect your walls from inevitable splashes and will provide an easy-to-clean, hard-wearing and attractive surface. Even a ceramic splash back above the basin or around the bath will smarten up the room and help keep it that way.

Bathroom tiles are especially practical when matching accessories like soap dishes, toothbrush holders and towel rails are included in the tile range.

The choice of tile designs is vast – from expensive, artist designed murals, to colours and patterns specially made to co-ordinate with current sanitary-ware. Of course, there's nothing to stop you from creating your own designs by mixing plain tiles (sometimes called 'field' tiles) with patterned ones.

Ceramic tiles can be matt or glazed – for a bathroom it's best to pick the glazed type which come in several sizes. The majority of tiles are square – 108mm(4¼in), 150mm(6in) and 200mm (8in) being the most popular – but you

can also get rectangular tiles and special border tiles for finishing off.

Ceramic tiles can be successfully fixed to virtually any flat, sound surface: plaster, plasterboard, blockboard, plywood or chipboard – even old tiles if you want a change of design.

Since the introduction of the universal tile, tiling has become much quicker and easier. Universal tiles have at least two glazed edges so you don't have to order any old-fashioned round-edge or corner tiles, and the edges taper slightly making them self-spacing – you can just butt them up together without the need for fiddly spacers.

If square-edges tiles (left) are used, they may need spacers; universal tiles (right) can be butted together.

Checklist

Tools
25mm × 25mm(1in × 1in) battens
spirit level and try square
measuring rod of 50mm × 25mm
  (2in × 1in) softwood
plumb bob and hammer
notched spreader
tile cutter and tile pincers
sponges
carborundum stone
wooden dowel
spacers (if required)

Materials
cellulose filler and sugar soap
tiles and adhesive
grout and silicone sealant
50mm (2in) masonry nails (solid
  walls) or 50mm (2in) oval nails
  (plasterboard walls)

What the job involves

Tiling a bathroom is time-consuming but it isn't difficult provided you have the patience to prepare a sound, flat surface and maintain level, even spacing. You won't go far wrong if you adopt the following procedure.
● Prepare all the wall surfaces; they must be reasonably sound, dry and free from grease.
● Mark off a wooden batten in divisions of one tile height and draw a line on the wall marking the top of the area you want to tile.
● Mark the position of the bottom of the last row of full tiles by drawing another horizontal line on the wall. Nail a batten against the line.
● Plan the tiles across the width of the wall and draw a vertical line marking the last row of full tiles – aim to have cut tiles down the sides of internal corners. Fix a batten against the vertical line.
● Spread an even layer of adhesive on the wall and start laying the tiles.
● Lay all the whole tiles.
● Measure, cut and fit the remaining border tiles.
● Grout the tiles, sponging into joints.
● Fill gaps between the tiles and the bath or basin with sealant.

BEFORE YOU START . . .

● Estimate how many tiles you require by dividing the height and width of each area in turn by the size of tile you want and multiplying the figures together (see diagram below). Allow for cut tiles by counting each as a full tile.
● Check with your tile supplier what type of adhesive is recommended for use with the tiles you have decided on.
● Buy sufficient grout for the job. Consider buying a coloured grout – there are many colours to choose from and the effect can be startlingly original.

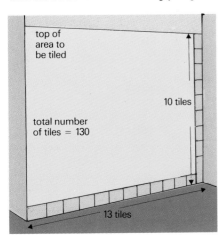

Estimate each area to be tiled separately. Allow for cut tiles by counting them as whole tiles

WATCH OUT FOR . . .

● Unstable or bumpy walls. Walls in very bad condition may have to be replastered or lined. Painted or tiled surfaces should be checked for soundness and must be sanded to provide a key for the adhesive. Wallpaper must be stripped off completely.
● Walls out of true. Never assume that walls, floors, ceilings and fixtures are perfectly level and flat – always use a level starting point.

Prepare the surface

Leave new plaster to dry out for at least four weeks before attempting to tile over it. Old but sound plaster should have all cracks and depressions filled before sanding down. If the wall is in very bad condition you will have to completely replaster it. Strip off all

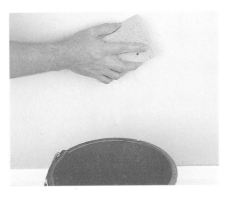

Strip off wallpaper, wash the area to be tiled with sugar soap, score surface with sandpaper

wallpaper no matter how firmly it's stuck down. Any moisture trapped inside the wall – or even from the tile adhesive – could cause the paper to peel away at a later date, taking the tiles with it.

It is possible to tile over paint provided it is not flaking. If the paint is sound, wash it down with a sugar soap solution to get rid of any greasy patches, then score the surface with sandpaper wrapped around a sanding block to provide a key for the adhesive.

When the walls have been prepared, make a measuring rod by marking a long wooden batten into tile divisions, remembering to allow for the grouting gap between each one if you are using spacers. The easiest way to do this is to lay a row of tiles on the floor, (insert spacers if you are not using universal tiles) and to mark off the rod directly from the tiles.

To make sure your first row of tiles is completely straight, draw a horizontal line on the wall marking the top of the area you want to tile – the ceiling or half-way up the wall.

TIP . . .

Ceilings are rarely truly horizontal. If yours is uneven or slopes at an angle, it is better to cut an additional row of tiles to ensure a good fit. Always draw a level horizontal line at the top and work vertically downwards.

Using your rod, measure from the line down to the bottom of the area you want to tile – the floor or the edge of the bath or basin. The chances are that you will

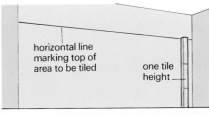
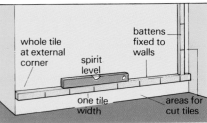

Determine where you are going to put cut tiles, then nail up horizontal and vertical battens

have to fill the bottom row with cut tiles.

Draw a line on the wall to mark the position of the bottom row of complete tiles. Check that it is horizontal, then nail a wooden batten along it the same length as the row.

Tiles are unlikely to work out exactly to the width of your room so you will have to have rows of cut tiles up the sides too – aim to run rows of cut tiles evenly up each side of an internal corner and to fit full tiles around external corners. It's worth bearing in mind that when tiling around an external corner, one row of vertical tiles must overlap the tiles on the return wall – make allowance for this and for the least obtrusive overlap when you are marking out.

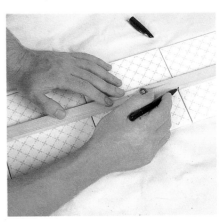

Make your own measuring rod by accurately marking off a straight batten into tile divisions

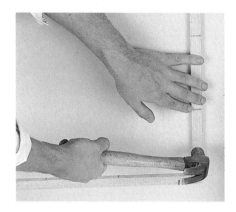

Before nailing up the vertical wooden batten, check that it is plumb and square to the base batten

When the position of your tiles has been decided widthways, mark out the horizontal batten. Where you are going to have cut tiles running vertically up the wall, mark a line and nail up a batten. Check that it is plumb and at right angles to the horizontal batten.

Fixing the tiles

Spread adhesive – use a notched spreader – in the corner where two battens meet at right angles.

Start laying tiles within your batten framework, working outwards in a triangular pattern and butting the edges of the rows hard up against the battens. Universal tiles can be laid edge to edge, but others have to be evenly spaced using matchsticks or spacers.

When you reach a fixture, go as far as you can with whole tiles then leave gaps to be filled later with cut tiles.

Continue until you have covered most of the wall.

1. Spread the adhesive thickly in the area where the two battens meet

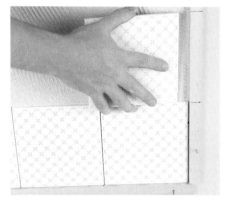

2. Position the tiles as tight as possible against the battens

Tiling the borders

Never assume that a wall is vertical or even; each edging tile must be individually measured and cut before fixing and moving on to the next one.

Start with the bottom row and work up the sides afterwards, making sure the grout lines match up with those of the complete tiles.

1. Remove the battens and measure each tile to be cut, allowing about 3mm(¹/₈in) for the grout

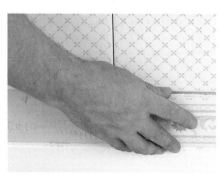

2. Spread adhesive on the wall and press the cut tile in place

TIP . . .
If marking, cutting and fixing each tile is tedious, speed up the operation by preparing the tiles in batches, of no more than six at a time, remembering to number each one to show where it is to be positioned on the wall. Tiles must be measured and marked individually.

Awkward areas

An awkward or irregular shape can be marked on a tile by drawing the shape on a piece of card first then transferring the image to the tile.

Score the outline and 'cross-hatch' the waste area with a tile cutter then nibble the waste away with tile pincers or ordinary pliers. Use a carborundum stone or a purpose-made tile file to smooth the edges.

TIP . . .
For delicate cuts, a tungsten carbide rod saw held in a hacksaw frame is the easiest and most accurate method.

To tile round a light fitting, turn off the electricity at the mains, unscrew the faceplate and cut tiles to the edge of the metal box fitted to the wall. Cutting does not have to be exact provided you make sure there is plenty of room for the faceplate and wires to go back easily. Grout the joints (see Finishing and grouting) behind the faceplate before screwing the faceplate back into place.

If you want to tile around a recessed window, first tile the wall flush to the

Make a card template if you have to cut a tile to fit around an awkward shape or obstruction.

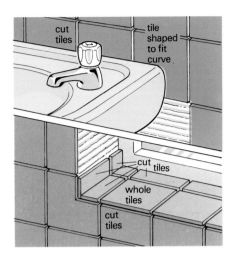

Basins, baths and recessed windows can present problems – use a rod saw to shape curves

edge of the recess, then spread adhesive on the ledge and start laying the tiles. The important thing to remember is that the tiles in the recess should overlap the tiles on the wall (in much the same way as around an external corner).

If the recess is more than one tile deep, ensure that the cut tiles are placed towards the back. When it comes to tiling the sides of the recess, double check that the grout lines are aligned with those on the wall. If you want to tile the underside of the recess, employ a slightly different technique: apply adhesive to the back of each individual tile before fixing it in place. To stop the tiles on the underside from falling off, hold them in place with tape.

If you are tiling over existing tiles which only come half-way up the wall, stagger the joints and overlap the existing tiles by 25mm(1in), then fill the gap with plaster and finish off at the top with quadrant tiles or wooden beading (see diagram column 1 below).

Fitting the accessories

Some accessories are fixed using screws and plugs, others with adhesive. Both types are available in standard tile sizes so that they can be incorporated into an overall pattern. Recessed fitments (like some soap dishes) may require an appropriately sized hole to be cut in the wall.

The screw-on type of fitment should be fixed only after the tiles have been up for 48 hours or more. Most of these fittings have predrilled fixing holes and are easily put in place.

Lightweight accessories like toothbrush holders are usually just fixed with adhesive like ordinary tiles but it's worth securing them with tape to the surrounding tiles until the adhesive sets.

Perhaps the easiest type of accessory to fit is the sort that is fixed superficially on top of the tiled surface. These are recommended by some tile manufacturers and are usually sold in kits which include special adhesive. This is applied to the back of the accessory which is then positioned centrally on a tile. Check that the

accessory is plumb, then tape it in place while the adhesive sets – the setting time varies but usually it takes about four hours (check any instructions).

Finishing and grouting

In a bathroom, it's only worth using a waterproof grout – quite apart from the persistent splashings and soakings, the condensation can ruin ordinary grout.

Wipe the grout over the face of the tiles, rubbing it well into the joints with a damp sponge. Wipe away any excess grout with a dry sponge as you go. After about 20 minutes – when the grout should still be soft – rub along the joints with a rounded dowel. Avoid touching the grout with your hands, and wear rubber gloves if you have sensitive skin as the alkali in the cement could irritate it. After a couple of hours, wipe off any dry grout you have missed.

TIP . . .
Cover the floor and sanitaryware with newspapers or sheeting when applying grout – especially if it is coloured; grout can be hard to remove once it has set.

Seal the gap between the tiles and the bath or basin with a silicone sealant – don't use plaster or putty. Make sure that the surfaces are dry and free from dust. Cut the nozzle of the sealant tube to match the gap then squeeze.

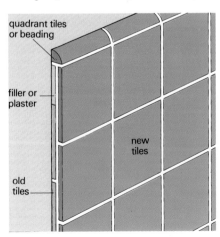

Overlap existing tiles, then backfill and finish off with quadrant edging tiles or a decorative beading

Tape accessories, especially heavy ones, in place until the adhesive has set hard

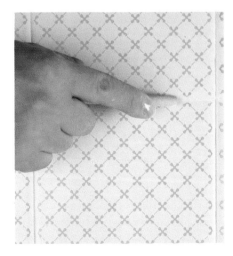

Sponge grout into the joints and wipe away any excess. Rub over the joints with a dowel.

ENERGY SAVER

No-one actually wants to waste energy, especially when they are having to pay for it, so running an energy-efficient home is a highly desirable goal for all of us.

For the millions of people living in older properties, the battle continues to improve insulation levels and keep heating bills under control. In this section you will find essential information on heating controls, insulation and double glazing, and also how to tackle the problems caused by that scourge of modern living, condensation.

Coping with condensation

Air always contains a certain amount of water vapour, and the warmer the air is, the more moisture it can hold. If you chill warm moist air, it can't hold the vapour any more and deposits it as tiny water droplets called condensation. When it occurs indoors it tends to form on the coldest surfaces – like window glass, metal window frames, ceramic wall tiles and cold exterior walls. If it happens every day, air-borne mould spores will settle on these damp surfaces and begin to multiply, causing tell-tale black or brown stains on windows and walls.

Condensation and mould growth aren't just an eyesore; the mould makes rooms and clothes smell musty and can also be bad for your health, and worse still, the moisture can eventually soak into the fabric of the house, causing structural faults and heat losses.

You can actually do a lot yourself to cut down on condensation in the home. Here are some examples:
● Close the doors of steamy rooms such as kitchens and bathrooms while cooking, washing or drying clothes, so that moisture can't easily reach other parts of the house. Open the window (and close the room door behind you) when you've finished, to let the warm moist air escape.
● Make sure that tumble driers are vented to the outside air, using flexible ducting. Poke this out of an open window or, better still, connect it

permanently to a hole in the wall fitted with a grille to prevent rain penetration.
● Never block up airbricks and ventilators – they're vital for air circulation, and also help to get rid of moisture-laden air.

Air bricks are especially important in rooms containing fuel-burning appliances; without adequate ventilation they will burn inefficiently, and may produce noxious fumes. If you are unsure about whether you have enough ventilation for an applicance, consult your fuel supplier for advice.
● Try not to use paraffin heaters for heating – each pint of paraffin burnt creates a pint of water vapour. If you have no central heating, electric convector heaters are far more efficient, and need not be run continuously to provide adequate background heating.
● Sleep with your bedroom windows or doors open slightly for extra ventilation.
● Mop up moisture regularly from condensation blackspots such as window sills, tiled walls and shower cubicles (leave the door open to encourage air circulation). To discourage mould growth, wash down these areas regularly with a proprietary fungicide or diluted household bleach.

Improve ventilation

In problem rooms like kitchens and bathrooms, you need controlled ventilation to get rid of the steam produced by activities such as cooking and laundering clothes. The best way to do this is by using an extractor fan or ducted cooker hood (recirculating types will remove smells but not water vapour). You can fit a fan in the window, the wall or the ceiling, and it can be ducted to the outside air quite easily if your room has no suitable outside wall.

If condensation is a severe problem in these rooms, connect your fan to a device called a humidistat. It detects when the air humidity is rising, and turns the fan on automatically (and off again once the humidity has fallen). In bathrooms, it may be more effective to link it to a time switch, so the fan will run for about 15 minutes after the bathroom has been vacated.

Improve insulation

By keeping cold surfaces warm, you'll get less condensation. Double glazing will cut down condensation on problem windows. Sealed units are better than secondary glazing, since moist air cannot get between the panes, but even plastic film double glazing will bring some improvement. Replacement windows with metal frames must incorporate a thermal break in the construction, otherwise condensation will still form on the cold frames.

On cold exterior walls, use 'warm' decorating materials like cork, blown vinyl wallcoverings (such as 'tile-on-a-roll' types) and paper-backed fabrics. They will help to keep the heat in. In serious cases of condensation, it may be worth having affected exterior walls dry-lined with insulating plasterboard, or even having cavity wall insulation.

Improve the heating

If you keep the air in your home warmer, it can hold more moisture and so less water vapour will be deposited as condensation. Of course, this will mean higher heating bills, so compromise by setting your heating controls to provide continuous low-level background heating, even in unused rooms, rather than the traditional morning and evening burst. Supply additional heating in problem rooms, using appliances such as convector heaters and oil-filled electric radiators that do not give off additional water vapour.

Buy a dehumidifier

If these measures don't cure your condensation problems, consider using a portable electric machine called a dehumidifier which can be moved from room to room as required. It dries and warms the air, collecting the moisture in a reservoir which must be emptied periodically. However, dehumidifiers have two drawbacks: they can be noisy – too obtrusive to run overnight in a bedroom – and are relatively expensive at around £300-£400. But as a last resort, they often provide a permanent solution to the problem.

CONTROLLING CENTRAL HEATING

Lack of control over your central heating system means money down the drain in wasted energy. Here's how to understand the controls you've got, what they do and how to use them wisely. Once you know, you'll also be able to improve, repair and update your own system.

Central heating systems, even new ones, tend to be fitted with the barest minimum number of controls – and often with the cheapest and least responsive type. This means they're often running inefficiently, either by giving out heat where and when you don't need it, or by not heating particular rooms adequately or economically.

On the other hand, if you've just had central heating installed or have recently moved house, it's likely that the heating system you've inherited is a mystery to you. It may be designed for different requirements and fitted with controls that don't offer you what you want, or you may simply not understand how to regulate the various components. This means that you're not getting the best from your heating.

Improving your system
If you find your system inconvenient or expensive to run, don't worry – it's possible to adjust and improve the

Your programmer is the most obvious control item for your central heating but it's not the most important. Pumps, valves, thermostats and the system into which they fit exert a greater influence

controls that govern it to obtain a more balanced performance. And you'll probably make substantial savings in running costs into the bargain.

But before you begin tampering with the controls, you'll need to get to know your heating system and how it all fits together – and you'll also need to be able to recognize the type of controls already in use. Understanding exactly how wet central heating works is the first step. Understanding how controls allow you to get the greatest comfort and convenience from your particular system is the second.

Understanding central heating
The most common form of central heating is fuelled by gas or oil and is called a 'wet' system. The basic theory is quite simple, but there are many different types of system and the controls that govern them will vary. Compare your system with that shown in the schematic illustration (below) of an ideal fully automated type; in doing so, you'll discover if and when there's room for improvement. The following points should help to put things in focus.

At the heart of the conventional system is a **boiler** which heats up water supplied from a small tank in the attic (called a **feed and expansion tank**). The hot water is then pumped through pipes and **radiators** (or other heat emitters) to

distribute its heat evenly throughout the house. As the water flows through the radiators it cools and returns to the boiler for reheating and recycling.

As well as flowing between the boiler

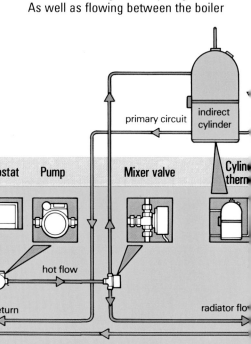

HEATING CONTROLS AT A GLANCE

cold tank

typical automated central heating

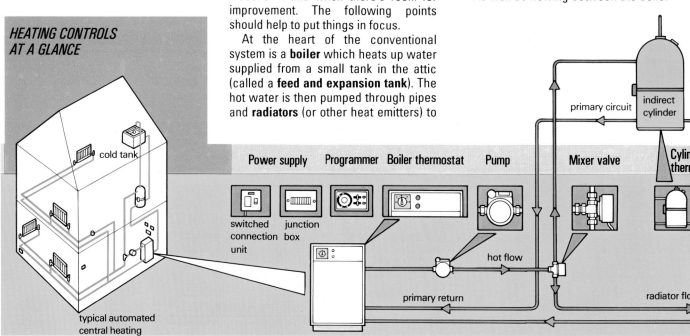

Power supply	Programmer	Boiler thermostat	Pump	Mixer valve	Cylin therm
switched connection unit	junction box				

primary circuit

indirect cylinder

hot flow

primary return

radiator flo

The pump

A pump helps the water to circulate around the pipes and heaters – it's electrically connected to the **programmer** and to the boiler so that it knows when to go on and off. It may be fitted to the flow or return pipe close to the boiler, though some are integral to the boiler itself.

Most central heating systems are fully pumped – water is pumped round the heating and the primary circuits. Even without the aid of a pump, water would flow round the circuits by natural gravity – hot water is lighter than cold so it tends to rise as cold water displaces it. This is called a **'gravity flow'** and is often used on the primary circuit, but only when the cylinder is directly above the boiler. And because gravity flow is slow, the pipes must be bigger to offer less resistance, so heat is lost before it reaches its destination. Thus, a pump speeds up the heat output, allows smaller pipes to be used, reduces heat loss and makes the system more responsive. If it breaks down, the boiler will continue to operate but the hot water will not travel around the system (beyond a limited gravity flow effect). They are not difficult to replace.

Importance of controls

The controls are a vital part of this and any other heating system; you need the right amount of heat, where and when you want it. Controls do just that. **Thermostats** help you to get the right amount of heat from the various elements in your system; **timers** and **programmers** help you to select the times when the heating and hot water comes on and off; **valves** and the **pump** control where the hot water, and therefore the heat in the system, goes to.

Programmers determine when your heating comes on – some systems allow separate settings for the hot water circuit

Boiler controls

Gas and oil boilers are controlled by integral electrical thermostats – they're part of the unit you buy. The thermostat keeps the water inside the boiler's heat exchanger at a constant, preselected temperature – the burners ignite as the temperature falls and are extinguished when the water reaches the preselected temperature.

Modern boilers are usually designed to run radiators at about 80°C (176°F), but in mild weather the boiler temperature should be reduced slightly to prevent internal corrosion.

If, on the other hand, the heating seems to be unable to cope with severe weather, turning the boiler up to 90°C (194°F) gives a far greater heating capacity at all the radiators – their maximum heat output is governed by the boiler's running temperature.

and radiators, hot water also flows from the boiler to a coil inside your **hot water storage cylinder**. The hot water in the coil heats up a separate supply of cold water coming from the main tank in the attic. It is the water stored in this cylinder – heated by the hot water flowing through the coil – which supplies all the taps throughout the house. The water from the coil returns to the boiler for reheating as it cools down – this flow between the boiler and the cylinder is known as the **primary circuit**.

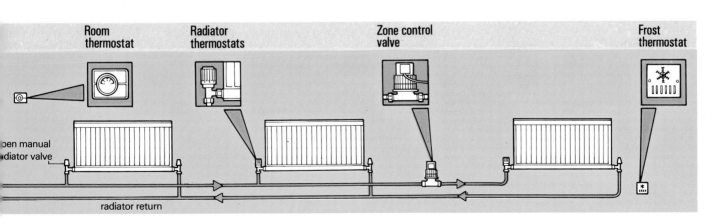

Room thermostat | Radiator thermostats | Zone control valve | Frost thermostat

open manual radiator valve

radiator return

It's unwise to set the boiler thermostat below 60°C (150°F) because this tends to cause condensation which will corrode the heat exchanger.

On cruder conventional, systems, the boiler thermostat setting also determines the temperature of water stored in the cylinder. This arrangement has three serious limitations.

First, when the heating is switched on, the domestic hot water in the cylinder is automatically heated to the same temperature as the radiator circuit. When you consider that a comfortable bath temperature is about 43°C, you'll realise the dangers of scalding, especially if young children, the old or infirm are in the house.

Second, a high water temperature in the cylinder will cause scale deposits to form inside, especially in hard water areas. This can lead to discolouration of the tap water and to blockages.

Finally, when the heating is switched off, the boiler will remain hot all the time the domestic hot water circuit is switched on. Even if the cylinder is full of hot water, the boiler will keep igniting under instruction from its own thermostat. Because the boiler itself is not insulated this cycling effect will continue as heat escapes through the flue and casing. What the system needs is a means of telling the boiler that the cylinder is hot enough and a way of diverting heat away from the cylinder.

Cylinder thermostats

A cylinder thermostat allows you to

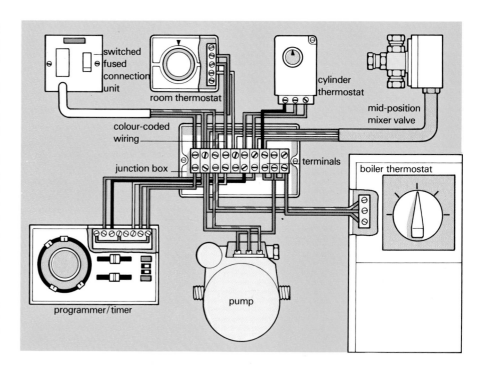

Most control components link at the junction box, which forms the heart of the electrical control connections

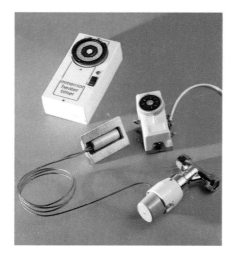

Hot water can be regulated by cylinder thermostats. An immersion can be independently controlled

choose a lower temperature for domestic hot water than that dictated by the boiler/radiator circuit. There are two types; an electrical thermostat, or a mechanical valve attached to the primary pipework.

An electrical cylinder thermostat is strapped to the side of the cylinder and connected to the programmer and boiler. It senses the temperature of the water stored there and, when it's hot enough, sends a signal to shut off the boiler. However, this type is only effective as long as hot water only is required – as soon as the radiator circuits begin working, water temperature is again governed by the boiler thermostat.

The thermostatic cylinder valve type is better; the body of the valve fits on the return pipe to shut off water returning from the primary circuit, thus giving independent temperatures in the radiators and at the cylinder. A remote sensor taped to the cylinder governs the operation of the valve – when the water is hot enough, the valve closes and prevents water flowing round the primary circuit. Once fitted, there's little that can go wrong.

Room thermostats

A room thermostat senses the air temperature of the house, or a zone in the house, and sends a signal to stop or start the radiator circuit. Originally designed to be the sole form of air

temperature control, they were connected to the boiler and pump via the junction box. It's now very common to find more than one 'roomstat', each controlling the temperature of a zone of the house. In this case, they'll also be connected to a zone valve which opens when the zone 'roomstat' calls for more heat.

Roomstats must be sited in an optimum position to sense ambient room or zone temperature – away from localised draughts and localised heat (like a cooker or television set).

Single roomstats seem to have fallen into disrepute; partly because they're inflexible (all the rooms are under the one control) and partly because a central control makes radiator sizing (and therefore output) much more important to get right. Zone roomstats offer more control, but you'll need a zone valve for each roomstat.

Zone valves

A zone valve, in conjunction with a second roomstat, offers more local control than a complete heating system controlled by just one roomstat. The only fundamental requirement is that the pipework must be easily divided into separate runs. A careful examination of your system and its pipe routes will determine whether this is so. If the pipework branches to supply an upstairs and a downstairs circuit, a zone valve can be usefully employed to operate each circuit independently.

A room thermostat in each zone is the best method of control (governed by the programmer), but an additional time clock may be included to switch off upstairs circuits automatically.

Radiator valves

Thermostatic radiator valves (TRVs) provide an even more flexible local control than zoning and are much more easy to fit than a zone valve. The TRV fits between the radiator and its flow pipe to replace the conventional manual valve. Here it adjusts the individual radiator's output by opening and closing the inlet. More or less water respectively enters the radiator, thus compensating for temperature losses and gains.

TRVs are a relatively modern innovation and have been designed to replace manual valves without the need to change the supply pipework – a wise move on the part of the manufacturers. TRVs consist of two parts: the body of the valve replaces the existing manual valve on the flow side of the radiator and is connected to the radiator and pipe in the same way (a screwed joint into the radiator; a compression joint on the pipe). The sensor or actuator

Fitting thermostatic radiator valves

You can easily replace manual radiator valves with thermostatic valves on gas or oil-fired central heating systems, but don't fit them to solid fuel systems without seeking expert advice. However, it's essential that you leave at least one of the radiators with a manual valve always open so that the pump has an 'open' circuit when the radstats close down all the other radiators. Choose a radiator furthest from the boiler or in a central position (the hall, for example) for this purpose.

● You'll need two spanners, a bleed key, a radiator valve key and some PTFE tape. You may also need a hacksaw, file and wire wool.

Radstats only work when connected to the flow side of the radiators, so you'll need to establish which side is which for each radiator. To do so, turn off the system and allow it to cool, then turn on and feel the pipes on each side of each radiator. The flow side is the one that gets hot first – label it. While doing so, take note of any drain cocks fitted to the pipework – they'll come in handy later.

● You'll then need to drain the system. Turn the entire system off at the programmer or at the fused connection unit (or plug), then tie up the ball valve in the feed and expansion tank so that it doesn't allow fresh water to run into the tank.

Connect a hose to the lowest drain cock in the system – it may be below the boiler but it

1. Tie up the ball valve on the feed and expansion tank, then drain the system

2. Identify the flow pipe; you must fit the radstat on this side of the radiator

3. Remove the old manual valve; screw the new body into the radiator tapping

may equally well be somewhere in the pipework. Run the other end of the hose to a low point outside the house.

● Open the drain cock to empty the system. If you open all the bleed nipples on the radiators at the same time, the water will drain out more easily and quickly.

● When the system's empty, hold the valve steady and undo the nuts on the pipework and radiator. Remove the valve, and you'll see the threaded shank in the radiator inlet; remove this using a radiator valve key.

● Remove the nut and olive on the pipe by gently tapping the nut upwards until the olive is forced off. If that doesn't work, carefully cut through the olive, but watch that you do not cut the pipe.

● Check that the copper pipe is long enough to locate in the new valve body – if it's too short you may be able to pull it up slightly. If not, you'll need to

4. Carefully join the old pipe to the new valve with the compression joint

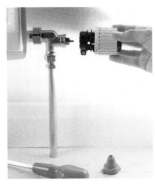

5. Attach the sensor to the valve body. Fill the system and check for leaks

cut the pipe lower down and add in a new section.

● Wrap some PTFE tape round the threaded shank of the new valve and screw it into the radiator inlet with the valve key. Connect the supply pipe at the bottom of the valve with the normal compression fitting.

● Remove the protective cap and attach the sensor or

actuator (if fitting the remote type, screw the sensor to the wall and attach the capillary tube to the valve body).

● Refill the system with the radstats fully open, bleed airlocks (start with radiators lowest in the system) and check for leaks. Restart the system and repeat bleeding for fresh airlocks.

Wall thermostats control room heat, setting the boiler and pump in motion during the 'on' periods. A 'froststat' is a safety device designed to turn on the heating automatically when the temperature reaches 4°C

attaches to the valve body; when the preset temperature is reached, it closes the valve inlet so that the radiator begins to cool down. When the temperature falls below the preset level, it opens the valve and allows in more hot water from the boiler.

There are two types of TRV; one has a remote sensor at the end of a capillary tube, the other has an integral sensor. Those with integral sensors are less obtrusive, but those with remote sensors are more accurate because they are not affected by proximity to the radiator itself – they sense the air temperature nearby. You fit the valve body in exactly the same way, but its sensor is fixed to the wall – the capillary tube connects the two parts.

It's not a difficult job to replace ordinary existing manual valves with TRVs, but you must leave at least one radiator on an 'open' manual operation to stabilize the load on the pump and this also helps to reduce noise within the heating system.

TRVs, or 'radstats', can be used to provide individual radiator control, even in a system governed by a room thermostat – it increases the amount of local control at your disposal.

Frostat sensors

Low-limit thermostats, or 'frostats', are safety devices or sensors that are located in a part of the house which is most vulnerable to frost damage – for example, below the floor and attached to an external wall. The froststat only comes into operation if the temperature falls below a dangerously low level – generally 4°C (39°F) and will remain in operation until the temperature rises. It will also override all other controls. They're particularly recommended for use in systems which may be left off for long periods in cold weather or in houses in exposed conditions.

A device called a compensator has a similar function; it is an outdoor sensor intended to forewarn the system of changes in conditions outside the house. It's only really effective in houses that are badly insulated and in which the inside temperature would change rapidly as outside temperature changes. A compensator makes little sense in today's well-insulated houses because it would be turning the heating on and off as the temperature outside changes, without the inside temperature needing any adjustment.

Timeclock controls

Central heating programmers are designed to control all the different components of a system, providing an automatic switching operation through a timeclock. The clock switches the boiler on and off and engages the roomstat at preset times. The roomstat then sends signals to the pump to increase or reduce the heat output in order to balance the air temperature.

Most programmes have a four-tappet clock so that you can set the heating to come on before you wake up and to go off when you leave the house, then to come on before you arrive home and to go off when you retire to bed. If you change your routine, there's generally an override switch for constant heating or an override selector which can 'jump' the preset 'off' positions.

Most central heating systems also provide hot water and it's not uncommon to want heating and hot water at different times of the day. With a gravity system, it's not possible to have heating without hot water, but it is possible to have hot water only and for the hot water and heating to go on and off as many times as the clock can manage. With a fully pumped system, it's possible to have a greater variety; hot water only, heating only, hot water and heating, permanently or at preset times.

The programmer may be the electrical centre for the central heating system and contain the junction box, or the junction box may be separate from it. In either case, it will be connected to the power supply via a 3amp fused connection unit or a plug and socket.

If you find that your programmer does not include enough variables, it is possible to upgrade it, but it's a job for a professional heating engineer.

THE VALUE OF INSULATION

Intelligent insulation can dramatically reduce your fuel bills but, if it's to save you money in the long run, you need to know what types are available and where they're most cost-effective.

There are many rules and regulations that ensure houses are built to sound structural standards, but it's only relatively recently that energy conservation has been taken into consideration. As a result, unless your house is very modern indeed, the heat losses could be quite alarming. With the right sort of insulation, you'll almost certainly be able to save pounds on your fuel bills.

But choosing the right sort of insulation really depends on the way your home is built, the way you heat it and the way you use it. It even depends on where in the country you live. But whichever type of insulation you consider, you have to ask yourself whether the cost of installing it can be justified by the likely reduction in the cost of heating your home.

Deciding priorities

To begin with, you have to decide at what point investment in insulation becomes worthwhile. There are a number of ways to work this out, but the easiest is the 'payback time' method. Simply divide the initial cost by the likely savings per year, to find out how long it will be before you show a profit. As a rule of thumb, if the answer is more than about five years, the investment is questionable. However, fuel prices do change and are unlikely to go down, so an apparently marginal investment now may turn out to be a very good deal in a few years' time.

It is easy enough to work out the initial cost of the insulation. Just shop around for materials if you are doing the work yourself, or get quotes from several contractors if you are hiring professionals. Working out the likely savings is a far bigger headache.

Many suppliers base their claims on figures from the Department of Energy. They assign a percentage of the total heat loss from a typical semi-detached house to particular causes – the roof,

The glass fibre particles in loft insulation wadding can be an irritant if breathed in. Always wear protective clothing while working – cover hands and face especially.

walls and so on. These figures are fine as a general guide, but don't be misled by them. Remember the figures are percentages of the **total heat loss**; not of your fuel bill. Even if you could completely insulate something responsible for, say, 10 per cent of the total loss, you will not cut your heating costs by 10 per cent – the reduction will be far less. Secondly, remember that unless you happen to live in a typical 'semi', the figures for your home may be wildly different. For example, while the heat loss due to draughts is around 10 per cent of the total of that lost from a typical semi-detached house, in a very draughty old house the true figure could be as high as 50 per cent

The heat-loss formula

To work out true savings for a complete house is a bit complicated and, in fact, for totally accurate results you need a

lot of time and a fairly good computer. However, given some research, a pencil, paper and tape measure, you can get fairly close. Basically, the amount of heat (in W/hour) that will get through a given part of your home's fabric depends on the area of that component (in square metres), its insulation value (known as the U-value), and the difference in temperature (in deg C) between the inner and outer surfaces. The formula is actually: U-value × temperature difference × area. You can find out the U-value for any component – from 25mm of plaster to a sheet of glass or a brick wall – by using builders' or architects' reference books (available at many reference libraries).

So let's suppose you are thinking of

double glazing a total window area of 10 sq m. Single glazed this has a U-value of about 4.3 which means even if the indoor temperature is just 1°C higher than the temperature outdoors, that window will waste 43 W of heat every hour. Double glazed, that window would have a U-value of just 2.5 giving you a saving of 18 W per hour. And how much is that worth in hard cash? Assuming you heat using electricity, that's easy – it's the cost of 18 divided by 1000 units: 0.018 kW/hr. You can find out the cost of a single unit from your local electricity board (see **DATAFILE**).

If you don't heat using electricity, see if your fuel supplier will give you an estimate of the cost of a 'useful' kW/hr. Alternatively, enquire at your local reference library. You will probably be able to manage the conversion from therms, sacks of coal, or whatever, for yourself. But remember to allow for the fact that only 70 to 90 per cent of the theoretical kW/hr equivalent can be counted as useful – burning fuel is not 100 per cent efficient.

Of course, in real life the temperature difference is likely to be more than 1°C, but by knowing the average indoor temperature, and asking the local Meteorological Office for the average winter temperatures in your area, it's easy enough to work out the difference.

So much for the theory of insulation. What about the practice? Have a look at the existing insulation and consider what can be done to improve it.

Insulating loft space

An uninsulated roof in the typical 'semi' mentioned above is likely to be responsible for about 25 per cent of the total heat loss. That's a lot of heat. In fact, no matter what kind of house you live in, insulating the loft space to keep in some of that warmth is almost certainly one of the best, most cost-efficient insulation investments you can make – and it's a fairly easy job to tackle yourself.

There are basically two types of material used and the most common is blanket insulation. This consists of glass fibre wadding, sometimes sandwiched between building paper, and is sold in rolls of various thicknesses and widths. For convenience, it's usual to choose a width that gives the best fit between the joists of the loft floor, and for good insulation it is generally recommended that the insulation layer be at least 100mm(4in) thick, although 150mm(6in) is better. Existing insulation will probably be just 25-50mm(1-2in) thick, and is worth topping-up.

The second type of insulation is the loose-fill type – probably mineral fibre, Vermiculite, or polystyrene beads. This is simply spread out over the loft floor between the joists, but since it's not as efficient as glass fibre, the layer ought to be at least 150mm(6in) thick. In practice, though, it is unlikely to be deeper than the joists. The other problem with loose-fill insulation is that it tends to blow about, so look for gaps and drifts in the insulation layer.

Insulation in the loft may be hidden behind boards or building paper. The loft floor may have been boarded over to conceal the insulation. Alternatively, insulation may have been built into the roof slope – it almost certainly will be in attic roofs and beneath flat roofs. In this case, expect to find glass fibre blanket laid between the rafters and concealed by the walls/ceiling. Elsewhere, glass-fibre or polystyrene insulation in the roof slope may be concealed behind building paper or boards lining the undersides of the rafters.

Vapour barriers

There are just a few other points to look for where insulation is concerned. First, check for a vapour barrier of sheet polyester or something similar on the house side of the insulation layer. This is unlikely to be present in old insulation, but it's a good idea nonetheless

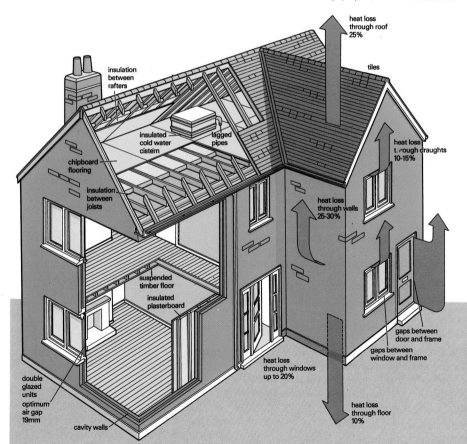

insulation between rafters

insulated cold water cistern

lagged pipes

chipboard flooring

insulation between joists

heat loss through roof 25%

tiles

heat loss through draughts 10-15%

heat loss through walls 25-30%

suspended timber floor

insulated plasterboard

gaps between door and frame

gaps between window and frame

heat loss through windows up to 20%

heat loss through floor 10%

double glazed units optimum air gap 19mm

cavity walls

HEAT LOSS AT A GLANCE
Heat loss may be by way of gaps and draughts around openings or by heat conduction through the material itself. Insulation has a greater effect if you assess your heat loss scientifically and judge the value of the insulation accordingly.

because it stops condensation forming within the insulation and thereby reducing its efficiency.

Secondly, check the lagging on any plumbing within the loft space. All pipes and tanks outside the insulation layer need protection to stop freeze-ups, particularly if they are close to the eaves. You should also check that there are gaps in the insulation immediately beneath water tanks. The small amount of heat leaking through here gives added protection.

The opposite is true for electricity cables – they should be laid **outside** the insulation to prevent overheating and to avoid the risk of fire.

The insulation must stop short of the eaves to leave room for ventilation which helps keep the loft space free of condensation. With loose-fill insulation you should use wooden baffles or proprietary fittings to stop the particles blocking up the eaves.

Insulating cylinders and pipes

Although the heat lost from an uninsulated hot water cylinder is unlikely to escape directly from your home, it's still expensive and wasteful. To reduce the loss, modern cylinders tend to have a built-in layer of insulating foam between 25 and 75mm(1-3in) thick. Older cylinders will probably be fitted with a quilted glass fibre jacket. In either case, adding extra insulation in the form of an additional or thicker jacket is still advisable. Don't worry about the effect this may have on the efficiency of your airing cupboard. Enough heat still gets through to air your clothes and linen.

The hot water pipes leading from the cylinder are unlikely to be insulated, but the heat loss from these is generally insignificant. There are just two exceptions to that rule. The first is where the pipes run through a particularly cold area – say, against an outside wall. The second is where there is a very long pipe run to a tap. These pipes should be lagged to stop the water in the run cooling to the point where it takes ages for hot water to emerge when you turn on the tap.

Heat loss through walls

A surprising amount of heat can escape through solid masonry. In fact, going back to the typical semi, leakage through walls can account for 25 to 30 per cent of the total heat loss. What has been (and can be) done about it depends mainly on the way in which the wall has been built – basically this means whether the wall is of solid or cavity construction.

Solid walls are very difficult to insulate economically so there is unlikely to be any existing insulation at all. If there is, it will probably take the form of glass fibre blanket laid between timber battens supporting a false plasterboard wall. Alternatively, insulation may have been added to the outside of the house. Rigid plastic foam is the material most frequently used, it's usually concealed behind tiles or some other form of cladding. More recently, a special render has been developed to provide the necessary weather-proofing.

Cavity walls are naturally better insulators than solid walls simply because of the air trapped between the two leaves of brickwork. However, in recent years their efficiency has been improved still further by replacing the inner leaf of brick with a leaf built from aerated concrete blocks or similar materials that provide both structural strength and extra insulation. Even so, quite a lot of heat still gets through, and the only way to reduce the loss still further is to fill the cavity itself with insulation. Two main types of insulation are common – plastic foam and mineral wool – both simply blown into the gap through holes drilled in the outer leaf. Plastic beads may also be used.

There is just one other type of wall you are likely to meet, and that is the timber frame construction. Here the wall consists of a timber framework lined on the inside with plasterboard, and on the outside usually with a single skin of brick. Insulation – probably glass fibre blanket – should have been inserted into the cavity when the wall was built. As this type of wall isn't really suited to injected cavity wall insulation, the only way to improve on the wall's natural ability to keep in heat is to treat it as if it were solid, although this is unlikely to be worth the trouble.

Insulating ceilings

Ceilings are unlikely to be insulated and, with the exception of those immediately beneath a loft or roof, they really don't need to be. That is, of course, assuming that the loft and flat roof are themselves adequately insulated. If they are not, and if it isn't possible to improve their insulation directly, it may be necessary to insulate the ceiling, as an alternative.

At the most basic level, the insulation may be nothing more than polystyrene ceiling tiles or something similar. Though, in fact, while this may help solve a condensation problem, it has little effect on heating bills. More serious attempts at insulation will take the form of a false ceiling – either a proprietary suspended ceiling system, or better still, a suspended plasterboard ceiling concealing a thick layer of glass fibre blanket.

Insulating floors

Although floors account for roughly 10 per cent of the heat loss from the semi, they are unlikely to have been specially insulated. The practical difficulties of tackling the job on an existing floor are too great to be justified by the likely savings. Instead, people have traditionally tended to rely on the insulation provided by floor coverings; a good quality carpet laid over a thick underlay is one of the best, and most easily installed, methods of insulation.

In the case of a suspended timber ground floor, however, additional insulation is occasionally added in the form of glass fibre blanket draped between the joists. But it's not very common. Laying it involves lifting every single floorboard, and unless this time-consuming job has had to be done for some other reason, to treat for wood beetle, for example, few people bother.

Insulation may also have been added to a solid floor, usually when it was first laid. This is done in two ways. One is to line the floor with a specially designed dense plastic foam and cover this with a thicker than usual screed. The other, far simpler method is to cover the screed with foam, and finish off with a 'floating floor' of chipboard. In fact, chipboard ready-backed with suitably dense foam is available for the purpose. It's doubtful if this is worth adding to an existing floor. To make adequate savings, you need to add about 50mm(2in) of insulation. So, allowing for the thickness of the chipboard, to carry out the job would mean raising the floor level by almost 70mm(3in). Just think of the problems that would cause.

Preventing draughts

Draughts through the doors and windows can account for 10 to 15 per cent of the total heat loss from the average semi, and anything up to a further 20 per cent or more can simply radiate through areas of single glazing.

The simplest and most economical remedy is draughtproofing. Even using fairly expensive materials, this should pay for itself in under two years. Various materials are used for the job. Fixed

gaps – those between fixed components of frames, and between the frames themselves and surrounding masonry – are generally filled indoors and out with a suitable flexible mastic or caulking. Gaps between the frame and opening doors and windows are filled using some form of draughtstrip. There are several types available, but the cheapest – plastic foam strip – is really suitable only for windows that are rarely opened, also loft trap doors, and the like. It simply isn't durable enough to take more than a modicum of wear and tear. Elsewhere sprung metal strips or plastic strips and rubber gaskets mounted on rigid plastic bodies are better. They last longer, too. Gaps beneath doors are also a problem and specially designed draughtproofing is needed – either a threshold strip fixed to the floor, or a rubber or brush strip fixed to the bottom of the door itself. The latter item is available in several forms, some cunningly designed to lift over door thresholds and similar minor

obstructions when the door is opened.

Whatever you find, or whatever you intend to use, check that it's in good condition and that all external doors and windows (including the loft trap door) have been treated.

Indoors, it's up to you whether you keep existing draughtproofing. It's certainly not worth adding any unless it's around the door of a room you use so rarely that you don't count it as part of the house for heating purposes. In fact, in adequately heated homes, a case can be made for removing interior draught-proofing. Internal draughts don't lose heat from the house as a whole and they do help ventilation – important if there are fuel-burning appliances which need a good air supply in the rooms.

Double glazing

As for the heat that escapes through single glazing, there is only one cure – double glazing. In other words, you add a second layer of glass to trap a layer of insulating air.

One system is sealed unit double glazing. Here both panes of glass are factory sealed, forming a single unit, and mounted in the window frame. This gives three main advantages. First, it means that windows can be opened as easily as if they were single glazed. Second, because the air between the panes is never disturbed, it gives maximum insulation and there is less risk of condensation forming within the air gap. If the condensation does form here, complain to whoever installed the double glazing. Finally, the thickness of the air gap is more likely to be close to the 19mm(¾in) optimum for thermal insulation. Its only real drawback is that it is best suited to specially designed new windows. Existing windows are unlikely to be thick enough to accommodate the air gap and second pane of glass.

Another popular double glazing system, secondary double glazing, is just as effective and it's easy to install yourself (see page 65, opposite).

Cold draughts around doors and windows can be cured with sealing strips, but leave adequate ventilation for heating appliances.

FITTING SLIDING DOUBLE GLAZING

Of all the materials commonly used in housebuilding, glass has the worst record for keeping heat in. Double glazing is the only practical way of cutting this heat loss, and there are now several relatively inexpensive double glazing systems on the market that are extremely easy for the householder to assemble and fit.

Double glazing works by trapping a layer of still air between two panes of glass or other glazing material. Air is a good insulator and as long as it stays still, very little heat is transferred between the two panes and so the rate of heat loss is greatly reduced. The optimum gap between the panes for efficient heat insulation is about 20mm (¾in); the insulation value drops quite noticeably with larger gaps, where convection currents in the trapped air can begin to circulate, and also with gaps of less than about 10mm(⅜in). It's interesting to note that sound insulation improves with a larger gap – 10mm(⅜in) is an optimum here – and with panes of different thickness.

There are two basic types of double glazing. You can either replace the existing glass with a sealed double-glazed unit – two panes of glass held apart by a metal or plastic spacer – or fit a completely independent second layer of glass over the inside of the existing window glazing. This latter method is known as **secondary glazing**, and is far more popular for treating existing windows. Installation is well within the scope of any do-it-yourselfer, and the job is quicker, easier – and cheaper – than fitted sealed units.

Once you've decided that you want to fit secondary glazing, your biggest decision will be in selecting which system to use. This article describes in detail how to fit **sliding panes** that can be left in place all year round. **Fixed panes** may be cheaper but are more incovenient for cleaning, for ventilation and, in emergencies, for escape. Secondary glazing systems are normally available in either aluminium or uPVC, with the aluminium types available in white or natural finishes; uPVC is the cheapest material, whereas aluminium is more durable. Systems with brush-type seals offer superior draught-proofing.

What the job involves

Installing secondary double glazing is quite straightforward as every system comes with detailed fixing instructions. All you have to do to get perfect results is to take accurate measurements at every stage.

To fit a sliding system you have to:
● Measure the overall indoor height and width of your windows.
● Buy the system components; most are sold in 'height' and 'width' packs, one containing all the vertical components of the system and the other all the horizontal ones. The packs come in unit lengths and you select the next size up from your actual window dimensions and cut it to size.
● Make up the track frame in which the double-glazing panes will slide, by cutting the extrusions to length and linking them together.
● Screw the track frame to the window frame itself, to the sides of the window reveal or to a timber sub-frame fitted within it – fixing methods vary from brand to brand and situation to situation (see diagrams on page 66).
● Measure and order the glass to match the actual track frame size, and

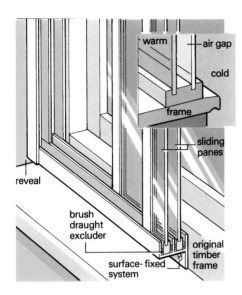

Surface-fixed systems are the least complicated to fit, although fitting screws can be fiddly

frame it with lengths of gasket and edge moulding supplied.
● Add fittings such as handles, catches and sliders, then lift the panes into place in the track frame.

BEFORE YOU START . . .
● Check the various brands of glazing systems which are available to see what minimum width of window frame is required for fixing the track framework. Most face-fixing systems need a frame width of about 25mm(1in), but some need as much as 42mm(1⅝in) others as little as 12mm(½in).

Checklist

Tools
tape measure
junior hacksaw
hand or electric drill plus bits
mallet
spirit level
bradawl
screwdrive
Materials
'height' pack of extrusions
'width' pack of extrusions
**corner pieces and screws (if sold
     separately)**
glass or plastic sheet

WATCH OUT FOR . . .
● Metal window frames, or very narrow wooden ones. It's best with both types to go for a reveal-mounted double-glazing system, or else to fit a thin timber subframe within the reveal, as close to the existing frame as possible, and to mount the track frame onto that.
● Protruding handles on opening casements and top lights. These may prevent you from fixing the secondary glazing as close to the frame as you should. If you can't replace them with slimmer fittings, go for a reveal-mounted track or fit a timber subframe to provide the necessary clearance.
● Out-of-square frames or reveals. With sliding secondary glazing it is essential that the track frame is square; if it isn't the panes will jam and the draught-proofing between panes and track will not work efficiently.
● Inadequate ventilation. The double glazing will cut off any ventilation that was obtained through poorly-fitted windows. If the room contains a solid fuel or gas-fired heater, make sure it has an independent air supply.

Alternative systems
Sliding secondary glazing systems with aluminium frames are generally the most expensive type on the market, and are trickier and more time-consuming to fit than other types. These alternatives fall into two main groups.

Fixed-pane double glazing ranges from the cheapest thin plastic film stretched across the frame on double-sided adhesive tape – to systems using magnetic strips, turn-button clips or simple screws driven through the pane surround. Permanently-fixed types suffer from the obvious drawback that they could block the ventilation and the fire escape route from a room if they were fitted to the only window.

Hinged panes are framed in plastic or aluminium extrusions, and are closed by simple catches so they can be opened in an emergency or for cleaning.

Preparation

Before you start the actual installation, it's important to carry out some preparatory work on the existing window to

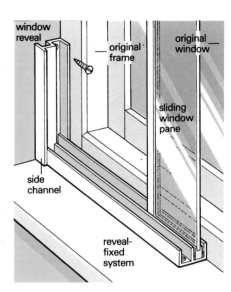

Reveal-fixed systems mean that the secondary glazing is neater and independent of the window

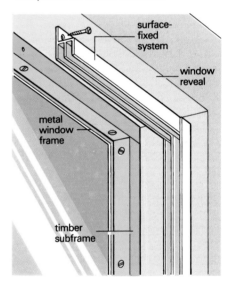

A timber subframe may be needed to clear protruding handles or if you have a metal window frame

ensure that the secondary glazing can work efficiently. The first thing to do is to ensure that the window is weathertight – in other words that there are no defects in the putty or in the glazing gaskets on modern windows. Make these good if necessary.

Next, fit draughtproofing round opening casements and top lights; it's no good having an efficient seal round the secondary glazing on the room side if the wind is howling into the air gap from outside. Now is the opportunity to redecorate the window if necessary, since painting it will be more difficult once the secondary glazing is put in position – in fact, you would have to completely remove the track frame to reach the inside of the window.

If you discover that you need to install a timber subframe within the reveal, cut and fit it next. Use timber of as small a section as possible for this, or use timber which matches the depth of the existing window frame, to preserve the window's appearance. You should have no problems fixing it to the sides of the reveal or across the existing sill, but the top may be difficult to secure if you have a metal or concrete lintel over the window. If you can't fix to the lintel easily, joint the head of the subframe securely to its sides and rely on the side fixings to hold the whole subframe securely in place. Before making the final fixings, check that the subframe is perfectly square and truly vertical; use packing pieces to position it correctly if necessary. Then fill any gaps and paint the subframe to match the reveal.

Fit draughtproofing strips to the casements to stop the air movement inside the new air gap.

Fitting the track frame

Follow the manufacturer's instructions carefully at this point, especially as far as taking measurements is concerned. Since every component has to be cut to size to fit your particular window, you have to subtract various figures from the overall window size to give the

different component dimensions. This means that accurate measuring and precise arithmetic are vital; always check everything twice and write your final figures down at every stage.

Cut the various track sections to length with a hacksaw, taking care to ensure that all the cuts are square. Remove any burrs from the ends with a file, then drill holes at the recommended spacings for the fixing screws.

Next, fit the frame tracks up to the window. With most types you have to fit the frame corners together first: if you do this, get someone to help you on wide windows – the frames aren't very rigid at this stage and you don't want to stress the corners.

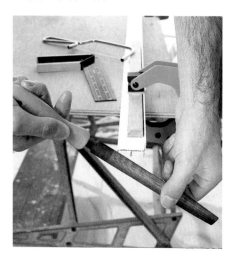

1. With the track cut to length, remove any burrs and square up the cut edges with a file.

2. Drill fixing holes in the frame at the recommended intervals – protect the frame finish with tape.

Use card or hardboard packing pieces where necessary if the frame doesn't quite fit, then mark through all the fixing holes with a bradawl. For direct fixing to the reveal you will have to remove the frame to drill and plug the fixing holes; with face-fixing types you can simply drive the screws straight into the wooden window frame. Check that the frame is square by making sure the diagonals are equal, and adjust it if it is necessary.

TIP . . .
On some face-fixing types the screw position can be awkward to reach. Either use cross-headed screws which you can offer up balanced on the tip of the screwdriver, or slip a short piece of clear plastic tubing over the screwdriver blade to hold the screw in place on the blade as you start to drive it in.

3. Hold frame up to the window; mark through the holes onto the frame with a bradawl. Screw frame into place.

Making up and fitting the panes

With the track securely in position, you can measure up for the glass. As before, follow the kit manufacturer's instructions here. Again, you usually have to subtract a set measurement from the inside track size, so double-check everything carefully so as to avoid mistakes. Most systems require 4mm

(³⁄₁₆in) thick glass with 'polished' edges but carefully check the instructions on this point too.

The next step is to measure and cut to length the flexible glazing gasket and the edge sections that frame each pane. As with the track, make sure your cuts are square, and file the ends of the edge section to remove any burrs.

Push the glazing gaskets onto the four edges of each pane, and check that the gap left at each end of the gasket is equal at all the corners; the corner pieces won't fit properly if the gasket gets in the way.

With the gaskets in place you can then add the edge sections. These are meant to be a tight fit, so carefully use a mallet and timber offcut to tap them into position over the glazing gaskets. Again, take care with the positioning to leave room for corner pieces. If the edges simply won't go on over the gasket, it may be that you have not prepared the gasket properly: some are only meant for 2mm(³⁄₃₂in) thick plastic sheet and then you have to remove certain sections of the gasket so that it will easily accept 4mm(³⁄₁₆in) sheet.

It's usually recommended that you fit the top and bottom edge sections first, then fit the corner pieces to each end of the first side section and tap it into place. Fit the remaining side section in the same way. Make certain at this stage that the edge sections are correctly placed as far as the integral draught-stripping is concerned. Check the instructions to make sure that all the

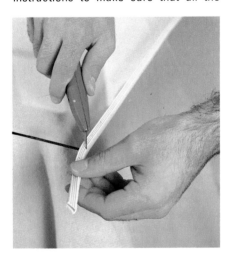

1. Fit the gaskets onto the glass – they just push on. Mitre-cut gaskets neatly to exact length

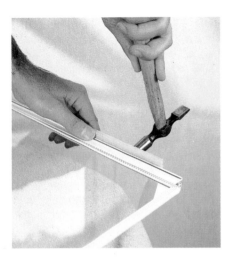

2. Tap on the frame edges once you've cut them to length. Spread the pressure with a wood offcut.

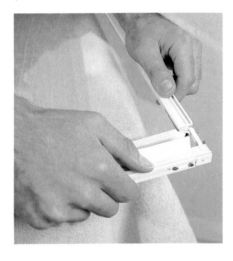

3. Add the corner pieces to the frame sides and tap the sides on. Secure corners with screws

sections are facing the correct way on the completed pane.

Most systems provide for a small handle on one edge of each pane, so slide this onto the appropriate edge section before fitting this to the pane – lock it in position by notching the aluminium at the desired level and tightening up the handle's screw. If the system has no separate handle, one of the vertical extrusions will have a handle moulded in.

With all four edges framed, go round the pane once more with the mallet to make sure the gasket and edge sections are all driven fully onto the glass edges. Before you lock the corner pieces into

place with the small self-tapping screws supplied in the kit, check that each is secure. Then tap the small PTFE sliders into the recesses in the lower corner blocks of each pane; these help the panes to slide smoothly in their tracks. Some systems have small rollers which screw to the bottom edge of each pane to carry the weight – these are particularly useful on tall windows, where the extra weight of the glass might make the panes stick.

Before fitting the panes into the track, clean the glass thoroughly on both sides to remove fingermarks. It's a good idea to clean the inside of the main window at this stage too. Then lift the first pane into place, offering up its top edge and engaging this in the inner of the two tracks before swinging the bottom edge inwards and allowing the pane to drop fully into position in the bottom track. Repeat the operation for the other pane which fits into the outer track, then check that they both slide smoothly and that the draught-stripping is sealing and doing its job properly.

As a finishing touch you can pin decorative wooden beading all round the reveal to disguise any bad joints in the track frame or gaps if you had to use packing pieces.

Options

If you have vertical sliding sash windows, horizontally-sliding double-glazing doesn't work very well. The panes would be very tall and narrow so they would tend to bind and wouldn't slide smoothly, opening and closing the sashes would be rather awkward, and the window would certainly look rather odd. A better answer is to fit a vertically-sliding secondary-glazing system instead.

With this type, each pane is held open or closed by means of a simple rachet in the side tracks, and because the meeting rails can be made to coincide with the mullions of the original windows the system is visually unobtrusive. The extrusions are usually uPVC rather than aluminium, which helps to reduce the weight of each pane.

CONSUMER ADVICE

A surprising number of laws and regulations apply to the householder and it is important to know your rights and obligations, especially if you are a keen DIYer. Going to court is a somewhat drastic remedy, however, and many problems can be sorted out amicably. So here are some alternative solutions for more minor disputes.

Always think carefully before getting involved in legal proceedings. Bear in mind that even if you win, going to court can be a very expensive business, and the outcome is never certain, so take a look at your options. Often disputes with neighbours are best sorted out over a cup of tea or a drink.

The police will not interfere in a domestic quarrel unless it is a criminal matter, although they may be willing to visit a neighbour who is causing a nuisance to several people – such as by noisy activities – and ask him or her to stop. This may be enough to put an end to the problem in some cases.

The Latent Damage Act 1986 enables you, in certain circumstances, to start negligence proceedings against builders, architects, surveyors and solicitors up to 15 years from the time that their unsatisfactory work was carried out, although in most cases shorter periods will apply. If the claim is for personal injuries, however, proceedings against builders, architects surveyors and solicitors should generally be brought within six years. Though in certain circumstances the time limits may be extended. Before taking any action decide first of all what it is that you want: repaired or replaced goods, compensation or damages (cash to pay for your losses and/or suffering) – or even just an apology. Getting cash may not be the answer in every case and this is often all that the law can provide. It may be far more productive to complain to the relevant trade association.

Seeking legal advice

If you decide that you really do need legal advice, visit a Citizens' Advice Bureau or Legal Advice Centre. The services provided by both organisations is free, and their staff can advise you on your rights and the law.

If you are advised that you must see a solicitor, you may still not have to pay a large fee. You can consult a Neighbourhood Law Centre (in many city centres); these are council-funded and are usually free, although you may be asked to contribute. Legally qualified staff are employed, and they can do everything that a firm of solicitors can, including taking a case to court. Many law centres specialise in particular branches of law, though, so you will have to ask if they will handle your case.

To find a solicitor, ask at a Citizens' Advice Bureau or at your local library for the Law Society List, which tells you what type of cases each firm handles, and the Legal Aid Solicitors List, which gives full details of firms willing to take cases for clients who are legally aided. Always telephone first and ask whether the solicitor can help with your particular problem, and remember to ask for an estimate of the cost.

Some solicitors offer 'fixed-fee interviews', whether you qualify for legal aid or not. This means that they will give you an inital half-hour consultation for a low, fixed rate. Any consultations after this are charged at the usual rate.

Green Form Scheme (Legal Advice and Assistance)

If you are of moderate means, ask if the solicitor's firm operates the Law Society's Green Form Scheme (not all do) which will help towards the cost of general advice from a solicitor. If they do, and you qualify, the first two hours of work will be paid for you and aid may be extended, depending on the circumstances. If you are on the borderline of the scheme, you may have to contribute towards the cost. And if you win money from the court, you may have to repay the Green Form Grant.

If the case goes to court (other than a civil case in the magistrates' courts), you must apply for civil legal aid. This, too, is means tested and before you are granted legal aid, the Legal Aid Office must be sure that it is *reasonable* for you to receive legal aid. If the case is one which does not merit the court's time, or if you have no chance of winning the case, you may not be given legal aid. You can appeal if you are refused legal aid, but there is little point unless some vital information was overlooked. If the court awards you cash damages but not costs, you may have to repay the legal aid grant out of the award money.

LEGAL PROBLEMS

It is almost inevitable that the home-owner will, at some time or other, be presented with a problem concerning his or her property – be it a dispute with neighbours over noise, the delivery of faulty goods, or confusion about the ownership of shared garden fences and responsibility for their maintenance. Here are some common problems, and advice about what you can do to solve them.

Maintaining fences

If your shared garden fence is falling down and your neighbour refuses to repair or even help to repair it, the first thing to do is to find out who really owns the fence.

Unfortunately it's not always so easy to establish who owns a fence or hedge although there are two rules of thumb. Generally, with a wooden fence, the owner of the garden on the side of the fenceposts is responsible for repairs. With a hedge and ditch, the owner of the hedge usually also owns the ditch and is responsible for its upkeep. That said, it is worth checking the house deeds (which will be with your bank or building society). These will sometimes specify who owns what, and whether anyone is under a duty to repair the boundary – in this case, a fence.

In some areas, such as London, there are regulations requiring house owners to keep walls and fences in good repair; if this does not apply where you live, however, the owners are quite within their rights if they refuse to repair the fence, unless they are actually endangering you or your property, or have covenanted the repair. If you really object to the disrepair of the fence, you will have to take action of your own to improve the situation.

One solution which will also help you to maintain good relations with your neighbours is to ask if you can repair the fence yourself, or offer to split the cost. Unless the deeds contain a term allowing access, you usually have no right to go onto your neighbours' land, even to repair your own property, without their permission. You may get a more helpful answer, though, if, as

suggested, you offer to share the work or the expense. It may be that they are refusing to help because they can't afford the repairs, or because they feel that you should contribute some way towards the cost – a long length of new wooden post and rail or chain link fencing is very expensive for someone on a low income.

Another simple solution is to disguise the fence by putting up a fence or wall of your own on your side of the existing fence. If you don't want to go to such lengths, train plants up the existing fence, or grow plants and bushes in front of it.

If all else fails, you could take your neighbours to court. You can do this if a local regulation or term in the deeds requires your neighbours to repair the fence. This is very much a last resort, as the case is likely to cost more than the fence. The council may be prepared to bring an action on your behalf if your neighbour is in breach of a bye-law or local ordinance, but if you are relying on deeds you will have to bear the cost of the case yourself.

Be warned that if there is any dispute as to the boundary – that is who owns the fence – the action may have to be brought in the High Court, which is extremely costly. However, you can take action in the County Court if the net annual rating value of the land does not exceed the court limit.

Complaints about noise

If you're a keen DIYer or craftsman, your neighbours may complain about noise from your shed or workshop. If this is the case, you need to know where you stand legally, as your neighbours may even threaten to sue.

Like offensive smells and smoky bonfires, excessive noise comes under the legal heading of 'nuisance'. To be actionable, a nuisance must be both persistent and unreasonable. This means that if you work late into the night, every night, your neighbours may well have a case, but if you only work on the occasional Saturday afternoon there may be nothing they can do. But if your behaviour does amount to a nuisance in

the legal sense, your neighbours can:
- Apply to the council for a noise-abatement notice, which may require you to make alterations to dampen the noise, or restrict working hours.
- Ask the local magistrate to issue a similar order.
- Sue you. If they sue they may get an injunction (an order from the court telling you to stop making noise) or damages (an order for you to pay them money). If you ignore a notice from the council or the court, you are committing a crime and can be fined or – if you defy a court order – sent to jail.

The simplest, and cheapest, solution of all is to be reasonable. If you are making enough noise often enough for them to sue, the simple answer is to be a bit more considerate. If you receive a letter from their solicitors, or a visit from the police, this should be enough to tell you that you've taken things far enough.

If you feel unable to modify the amount of noise you make, however, a helpful solution would be to soundproof your workshop. This is difficult to do and can be expensive if you aim for no sound to escape at all, but just fitting a carpet and lining the walls may help to dampen the noise. Fitting double glazing would help to cut down the noise, too, as well as keeping you warm in winter.

Soundproofing will not only make your neighbours' life more pleasant; it may also convince them that there's no need for a lawsuit.

If, despite all your efforts to limit your noise and soundproof your workshop, your neighbours still plan to sue, you need to seek legal advice. There are a number of possible defences to a nuisance charge – for example, that the 'nuisance' is part of the give and take of life or that the activity is to be expected in the locality. A greater level of noise would be tolerable, for instance, in an area of light industry. A solicitor will be able to help and advise you.

Faulty goods

Buying goods and finding that they are faulty once you get them home is a common enough problem. Happily, your consumer rights when faced with this problem are quite clear.

Whether goods are bought, leased or hired, they must be fit for their common, everyday use and for the purpose for which they are sold. They must also match the seller's description. Furthermore, if the goods are actually dangerous and damage results from using them, the supplier can be prosecuted – report the matter to your local Trading Standards Officer. You can also sue the supplier of the goods.

Before resorting to costly legal action, however, take the goods back to the shop. Any reputable supplier should replace them or refund your money without further argument. The only exceptions might be if a tool was sold as a 'second' and its defects were brought to your attention before you bought it.

If, for some reason, you are unable to sue the seller – for example, because you did not buy the goods yourself, you may be able to take an action against the manufacturer of the goods.

If the seller will not co-operate, go to a Consumer Advice Centre or Citizens' Advice Bureau. The seller may be more willing to help after a letter from one of these organisations. Neither organisation will take legal proceedings on your behalf but they may be able to obtain from the seller an offer of compensation – that is, a payment of the difference between the price you paid and the true value of the goods.

If this approach fails, consider suing the seller. For an inexpensive item this may be a waste of time and money, although if the item costs less than £500 you may use the small claims scheme in the County Court which is relatively cheap. You must bring the action within six years of the date of purchase and the court may award only the cost of repair, or compensation if the item is irreparable.

Remember that if you bought the goods by credit card you may be able to take action against the credit card company. There may also be the possibility of approaching a trade association, some of whom run arbitration schemes.

Basic services – your rights
Some country cottages and other properties in remote areas are not connected to the mains sewer; what's more, they may have no water, and

Hard facts: Disputes with neighbours

● **Gutters:** if your neighbour's are in such poor repair that water from their gutter pours onto your land, you can sue.
● **Trees:** unless a tree is subject to a council preservation order, you can cut back roots or branches that encroach on your land but you must offer the cuttings to the tree's owner. Take care not to leave the tree in a dangerous condition. You cannot go on to your neighbour's land in order to cut down the trees without his or her permission.
● **Children:** you are not liable for the actions of your children unless it can be proved that you were aware of what the children were doing and did nothing to stop it. You may, however, be liable if your

neighbour's children are injured by something on your premises if you know that they are coming onto your premises (even if uninvited). If you know that there is something dangerous on your property, it would be reasonable for you to do something about it.
● **Pets:** owners are not normally liable for the actions of pets unless they are aware that, for example, a dog is vicious and they do not take suitable precautions.
● **Bonfires:** it is illegal to light a bonfire in a smokeless zone, or to make 'dark smoke' (by burning rubber or plastics, for example) anywhere. However, the council may allow the occasional lighting of garden bonfires.

no electricity or gas supplies either. In such cases, contact the appropriate local board immediately. But beforehand, it's as well to know your legal entitlement to these services, which is as follows:

● If your property is not connected to a mains sewer, there should be a cesspit or septic tank. This should be emptied regularly by the council or a contractor but you must pay for this. If the cottage is near to a main sewer, you are entitled to be connected to it but you will have to pay for this. (If you are not connected to a sewer, the Water Authority is not entitled to charge you for sewerage too.)
● If there is no piped supply of water, you can demand to be connected to the mains, but once again, you pay – unless it is the council that insists on connection, in which case you need only contribute to the cost.
● If the house is within 45m (50yds) of an electricity main, the local electricity board is obliged to connect you but you may have to pay the cost of any line over 18m (20yds) and the part of the line which will lie in your own property. If there is no main nearby, you will need to club together with at least five other households in the same street; if you all sign a formal request for a supply, the

electricity board may be obliged by law to lay a new main.
● You have a right to be connected to a gas main that is within 23m (25yds) of your house, but you may have to pay for pipes over 9m (10yds) and those which lie on your property. If the main is further away, you have no right to be connected; if the gas board agrees to connect you anyway, you may have to pay the total cost.
● If it proves too difficult or expensive to arrange to be connected to the mains, there is a wide range of non-mains fuels and sewerage systems that you can use. Furthermore, any water that lies under your land and is not connected underground to the authority's supply is yours: if this is the case, you could fit a well or pump.

Refuse collection
Another potential problem for those living in out-of-the-way places is refuse disposal. If your home is not on the local refuse collectors' route, how can you get rid of your rubbish?

The district council has a duty to collect refuse but in many areas it need not collect more than one bin, and if the bin is so inaccessible that the cost of collection is prohibitive, they can refuse to collect. The council will collect bulky items but you must pay for these.

Take any rubbish that the council refuses to collect to the council tip, or dispose of it yourself. Much household waste can be burned (provided that the house is not in a smoke-control zone). Glass, metal and so forth can be taken to the council tip. The council are obliged to provide a public tip, free of charge, and can tell you where the nearest one is and when it's open. They are not obliged, though, to site the tip on the main road, so it may be a problem for you to get there.

Don't take rubbish down to the road-side and leave it there for the dustmen – this is littering, which is an offence. Leave it just inside your gate.

Sharing a garden
A dispute between leaseholding tenants over access to a shared garden is a common problem, but it is one that can usually be solved by the freeholder of the property. However, if the tenant who is denying access is also the freeholder, the problem becomes more complicated. Here's what you can do.

Arrange to meet with the freeholder and attempt to come to an amicable settlement of the problem. Even though you may feel there is no question of compromise, it may be preferable to a protracted and costly legal wrangle. Check your lease; if it entitles you to full right of access you should be able to enter the garden at any reasonable time, even if the access is via the other tenant's property. You should not have to ask permission to enter.

If the problem cannot be settled through discussion, you will have to direct a solicitor. If the other tenant is denying access unreasonably, as is probably the case, he will have little choice but to concede to the request for access – unless, of course, he is prepared for a court case.

You can apply through the court for an injunction to prevent him from block-ing your access but there are various reasons why this should only ever be a last resort. To begin with, injunctions of this sort can be very difficult to enforce, so you may end up not gaining very

Choosing a builder

When choosing a builder take as much care as you would choosing a new car or annual holiday. Try to ensure not only that the person you select is well qualified, but also that your contract with him provides some form of guarantee. Then if the workmanship or materials used proved faulty, you would have the necessary backing to make sure it was put right at no further cost to you.

First, look for a builder who is a member of a recognised builder's organisation, such as the Federation of Master Builders. Although this in itself does not provide a guarantee, it indicates that the builder is experienced and has agreed to abide by the rules and principles laid down by the Federation. Second, look for a Federation member who is also on the National Register of Warranted Builders. The Warranty Register is a scheme operated by the Federation of Master Builders in response to public demand for greater safeguards in the building industry. This demand arose following growing numbers of complaints and reported cases from members of the public about unsatisfactory and shoddy work carried out by 'cowboy' builders.

A leaflet providing further details of the FMB Warranty Scheme is available from the Federation of Master Builders whose address is listed in the Datafile section under the heading BUILDERS.

much. In addition, you may find that there are complicated clauses in the lease which affect the conduct of an official dispute between freeholder and so-called tenant. You may even find that you are obliged to pay all or part of the freeholder's costs as well as your own. And lastly, any official dispute (that is one that goes beyond a mere exchange of solicitor's letters) will be recorded and will be revealed during the search of the lease that will take place if you decide to sell. Such a revelation could discourage a potential purchaser.

Dry rot in a party wall
If you discover a patch of dry rot on a party wall and you suspect that it is coming through from the house next door, what action can you take if your neighbour is unwilling to put the problem right?

Dry rot is a serious problem that must always be treated quickly and by pro-fessionals. It occurs in untreated tim-bers in damp, badly ventilated areas and it can travel through masonry to infect other timber. Established dry rot takes the form of a large flat wrinkled fungus. This produces spores which quickly spread to surrounding timber. Once settled, fine grey threads sink into the timber and white gossamer-type growths are produced on the surface. This develops into the fungus and the process starts again. Specialist com-panies will not give a guarantee unless both sides of the wall are treated. These are dealt with as two separate jobs with each householder paying for his or her own treatment. But the law cannot force people to carry out treatment in their own homes. You may be able to sue if you can prove that your neighbour was negligent with repair work and the damp and rot are a direct cause of this. Dry rot may also be regarded legally as a nuisance.

If left unchecked, dry rot can cause serious damage, so try to persuade your neighbour that it is in his or her own interest to pay for treatment, before the situation worsens. If you are living in council accommodation, your local council are responsible: inform them immediately. Contact your landlord if you are a private tenant.

If your neighbour won't co-operate, you may be able to come to some agreement; perhaps offer to pay half the costs, or speak to your neighbour's relations who may be more sympathetic to the problem. Social services and environmental health workers cannot force entry or contribute in any way.

DATAFILE

These pages provide details of the recognised organisations and official bodies which you can contact when you need expert advice, information or specialist help in a particular field. If your query is about returning faulty goods, for example, simply look under *Consumer Advice*: if you need the services of a qualified electrician, find out who to contact for advice under *Electricians*. For quick and easy reference, subjects are listed in alphabetical order.

ARCHITECTS & SURVEYORS

Royal Institute of British Architects
Clients Advisory Service
66 Portland Place
London WIN 4AD
Tel 071-580 5533
Will provide list of RIBA members in your area, plus standard form of contract.

Royal Institution of Chartered Surveyors
12 Great George Street
London SW1P 3AD
Tel 071-222 7000
Will provide lists of building surveyors in your area.

BUILDERS

Building Employers Confederation
82 New Cavendish Street
London W1M 8AD
Tel 071-580 5588
Will provide lists of BEC registered builders in your area.

Federation of Master Builders
14-15 Great James Street
London WC1 3DD
Tel 071-242 7583
Will provide details about the FMB Warranty Scheme.

Institute of Carpenters
PO Box 111
Aldershot
Hampshire GU11 1YW
Tel 0252 21302
Will provide lists of registered members in your area.

CONSUMER ADVICE

Association of British Travel Agents Ltd (ABTA)
55 Newman Street
London W1P 4AH
Tel 071-637 2444

Citizens' Advice Bureaux
National Association of Citizens' Advice Bureaux
115-123 Pentonville Road
London N1 9LZ
Tel 071-833 2181
Will locate your nearest Citizens' Advice Bureau. Alternatively, local Citizens' Advice Bureaux are listed in your telephone directory.

Company Pensions Information Centre
7 Old Park Lane
London W1Y 3LJ
Tel 071-409 1933/4

Consumer Advice Centres
Deal with consumer complaints about products bought locally and local traders. Centres act as watchdogs for local authority Trading Standards and Weights and Measures departments.

Disabled Living Foundation
380-384 Harrow Road
London W9 2HU
Tel 071-289 6111

Electricity Consumers Council
Brook House
2-16 Torrington Place
London WC1E 7LL
Tel 071-636 5703

The Insurance Ombudsman
31 Southampton Row
London WC1B 5HJ
Tel 071-242 8613

Office of the Banking Ombudsman
Citadel House
5-11 Fetter Lane
London EC1A 1BR
Tel 071-583 1395

Office of Fair Trading
Field House
15-25 Breams Buildings
London EC4
Tel 071-242 2858

Office for Telecommunications (OFTEL)
Atlantic House
50 Holborn Viaduct
London EC1N 2HQ
Tel 071-353 4020
Will deal with consumer queries concerning phone bills.

The Society of Motor Manufacturers and Traders
Forbes House
Halkin Street
London SW1X 7DS
Tel 071-235 7000

ELECTRICIANS

See also **EMERGENCIES**

Electrical Contractors Association (ECA)
Esca House
34 Palace Court
London W2 4HY
Tel 071-229 1266
Will provide lists of members in your area, operates Guarantee of Work Scheme to put right faults.

Electrical Contractors Association of Scotland
Bush House
Bush Estate
Midlothian
EH26 0SB
Tel 031-445 5577
Will provide lists of members in your area, operates Guarantee of Work Scheme to put right faults.

ELECTRICITY

See also **EMERGENCIES** *and* **HEATING & VENTILATION**

Electrical Installation Equipment Manufacturers Association
Leicester House
8 Leicester Street
London WC2H 7BN
Tel 071-437 0678
Will provide information and literature on manufacturers of all kinds of domestic electrical fittings.

Electricity Consumers Council
Brook House
2-16 Torrington Place
London WC1E 7LL
Tel 071-636 5703
Publishes fact sheets and booklets on using electricity wisely, will investigate complaints on consumer's behalf.

EMERGENCIES

Blocked Drains
Contact local authority environmental health department if no local private firm can help. Try Yellow Pages first.

Electrical Emergencies
Contact local electricity board emergency number – listed in telephone directory under ELECTRICITY.

Gas Emergencies
Contact local gas board emergency number immediately – listed in telephone directory under GAS.

Locked Out?
Contact local police station if no locksmith can help.

Pests
Contact local authority environmental health department.

FIRE SAFETY

Fire Prevention Information and Publications Service
140 Aldergate Street
London EC1A 4HX
Tel 071-606 3757

GAS see **HEATING & VENTILATION** and **EMERGENCIES**

HEATING & VENTILATION

Confederation for the Registration of Gas Installers (CORGI)
St Martin's House
140 Tottenham Court Road
London W1P 9LN
Tel 071-387 9185
Will provide a list of registered installers

of gas equipment of all types (list also available at local British Gas showrooms and public libraries). Registered Installers also listed in Yellow Pages.

Electricity Consumers Council
Brook House
2-16 Torrington Place
London WC1E 7LL
Tel 071-636 5703

National Gas Consumers Council
6th Floor, Abford House
15 Wilton Road
London SW1V 1LT
Tel 071-931 0977
Publishes leaflets on using gas wisely, and will answer queries.

INSURANCE & SECURITY

British Insurance Association
Aldermary House
Queen Street
London EC4N 1TU
Tel 071-248 4477

The Insurance Ombudsman
31 Southampton Row
London WC1B 5HJ
Tel 071-242 8613

National Supervisory Council for Intruder Alarms
Queensgate House
14 Cookham Road
Maidenhead
Berkshire SL6 8AJ
Tel 0628 37512
Will provide a list of approved installers of burglar alarms meeting BS4737.

PLUMBING

See also **EMERGENCIES**

Institute of Plumbing
64 Station Lane
Hornchurch
Essex RM12 6NB
Tel 04024 72791
Will provide names from its register of plumbers in your area, does not guarantee members' work, but will investigate complaints on your behalf.

PROPERTY

Building Societies Association
3 Saville Row
London W1X 1AF
Tel 071-437 0655
Will provide useful leaflets on housing.

REMOVALS

British Association of Removers
3 Churchill Court
58 Station Road
North Harrow HA2 7SA
Tel 081-861 3331
Send SAE for helpful leaflet and names of local firms who are members. Will help to resolve disputes between members and the public.

SOLICITORS

The Law Society
113 Chancery Lane
London WC2A 1PL
Tel 071-242 1222

The Law Society of Scotland
26 Drumshaugh Gardens
Edinburgh EH3 7YR
Tel 031-226 7411

WINDOWS

British Plastics Federation
5 Belgrave Square
London SW1X 8PD
Tel 071-235 9483
Will provide information about uPVC window frames.

Glass & Glazing Federation
44-48 Borough High Street
London SE1 1XP
Tel 071-403 7177
Will advise on glass and double glazing; will also provide list of registered installers in your area.

Metal Window Federation
Suite 323-4, Golden House
28-31 Gt Pulteney Street
London W1R 3DD
Tel 071-494 4650

HOME MAINTENANCE AND REPAIRS

Every homeowner knows the importance of keeping his or her property in good repair. Not only does this keep the elements at bay, it also helps the property to maintain its value, which is obviously of great importance when you decide to sell and move on.

The chapter that follows deals with a wide range of both routine maintenance jobs and the sort of emergency repairs that can't wait until you next have a free weekend. There is information on everything from mending broken windows and clearing blocked drains, to repairing burst pipes, tackling damp and rot, tracing and curing electrical faults and stain removal.

Below is a handy checklist of basic tools and equipment that no well-prepared DIYer should be without. The list won't cover the tools needed for *all* the jobs you may want to tackle, but it should cover most everyday fixing and repair jobs.

Also listed are suggested items for stain removal kits (one for fabrics, the other for carpets) to keep in the home. Some of the items you may already have in your store-cupboard, others can be bought at most chemists, hardware shops and DIY stores.

A BASIC TOOLKIT

Electric variable-speed hammer drill
  plus twist drills and masonry drill bits
Extension lead on drum
Handyman's knife plus spare blades and
  a padsaw blade
Screwdriver – three for slotted-head
  screws (including a small insulated
  electrical screwdriver), plus Philips
  and Pozidriv cross-point types
Pliers with cutting jaws
Adjustable wrench or spanners (two)
Claw hammer
Small Surform block plane
Steel tape measure
Small spirit level
Tenon saw
Junior hacksaw plus spare blades
Filling knife
Portable workbench (eg Workmate)

ESSENTIAL ODDS AND ENDS

25mm (1in) oval wire nails
50mm (2in) round wire nails
Pack of assorted screws (No 8 and
  No 10 in various lengths)
Wallplugs
Cavity fixing plugs or toggles
Woodworking adhesive
Exterior quality filler (powder)
Frame-sealing mastic plus gun
PVC insulating tape
Pipe repair kit

FABRIC STAIN REMOVAL KIT

Biological pre-wash: excellent pre-soak remedy for many protein- and animal-based stains such as milk, blood, egg, and so on – but water mustn't be hotter than 60°C
Washing-up liquid, liquid detergents and ordinary soap bars: helpful on furnishing fabric stains
Eucalyptus oil: a traditional remedy for all kinds of grease and tar stains; also useful for sun-tan oil and curry stains
Laundry borax: an invaluable aid for removing grease and wine stains on cotton
Bleach: useful for whitening and deodorising fabrics. Domestic bleach is fine for cotton, but don't use it on wool or silk
Hydrogen peroxide: can be used safely on wool or silk. Sold in a 9 or 20 volume solution for home use
Ammonia: a useful alkali for removing dirt and grease; sold as a 10 per cent solution in DIY stores
Carbon tetrachloride: useful for removing grease and tar stains
Methylated spirits: the colour-free kind is a useful solvent for ball-point and felt-tip pen stains
Oxalic acid: can be used on rust and iron mould stains. But it is highly toxic and can be harsh. Buy a branded product

CARPET STAIN REMOVAL KIT

Carpet shampoo (dry foam type)
Branded solvent for grease and stain removal
Ammonia solution made up of 15ml (1tbsp) household ammonia to 250ml (1 cup) water
Methylated spirits (flammable, so store with care)
Laundry borax
Glycerine
Eucalyptus oil
Hydrogen peroxide
White paper tissues or kitchen towels

Reglazing a wooden window

Preparing the frame

Windows are a vital barrier against the elements but they're also fragile.

On most wooden windows, the pane of glass is held in a putty-lined rebate with triangular glazing sprigs or small panel pins. An outer layer of putty, angled to deflect rain, covers the fixings.

Some panes may be bedded in putty or mastic and held in the rebate with quadrant beading. Some top rails of sashes have a groove for the top edge of the pane. (Metal windows use a slightly different fixing method.)

When replacing window glass, measure the width and height of the rebate – at two or three points in case it's not square – double-check the dimensions, then order the pane (stating the width first) 3mm (⅛in) smaller to allow for movement in the frame, which could crack the glass. Order safety glass for low level glazing or panes in door frames.

For windows up to 1sq metre (10sq ft) use 3mm (⅛in) thick glass; 4mm (⅛in) up to 2.6sq metres (28sq ft); 6mm (¼in) for larger windows.

1. *Stick PVC adhesive tape over the broken glass in criss-cross fashion to contain the fragments*

2. *Tap out the majority of the broken glass gently from outside; wrap it up and dispose of it*

3. *Wear thick gloves to prise out the remaining shards of glass from the rebate by hand*

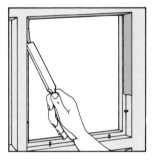

4. *Chop out the hard putty from the rebate with an old chisel, without damaging the frame*

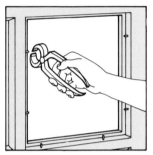

5. *Withdraw the old glazing sprigs or pins from the rebate using a pair of pliers*

6. *Clean up the rebate, sand it smooth, then apply wood primer by brush to the bare timber*

Fitting the new pane

To fit the replacement window pane you'll need a tub of linseed oil or dual-purpose putty plus some glazing sprigs or 19mm (¾in) panel pins, a light cross-pein hammer (which has a wedge-shaped pein opposite the striking face that's ideal for tapping in the fixings), and a putty knife for shaping the sealant to stop moisture penetration. Choose a knife with a flat blade and curved edges for shaping and mitring the puttied corners.

As a guide, allow about 125g (4½oz) of putty per 300mm (12in) of frame.

Putty may be excessively oily when you open the tub, so leave it open for a while to dry or knead the oil into the putty. Wet your hands prior to use so the putty doesn't stick to your fingers. Knead it until it is pliable.

Once applied, it's best to leave the putty for about a fortnight to form a skin, before you paint over it. Apply primer, undercoat and gloss, taking the final coat 2mm (¹⁄₁₆in) onto the glass as a seal against moisture penetrating behind the putty.

1. *Line the rebate with putty by squeezing it from your palm between thumb and forefinger*

2. *Press the new pane into the puttied rebate with your palms, pressing gently at the sides*

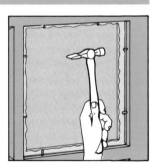

3. *Tap in sprigs or pins to hold the pane, sliding the wedge of the hammer across the glass*

4. *Roll putty into finger-thick sausages and press against the glass, covering the fixings*

5. *Shape the putty fillet to a bevel, mitring the corners using a wet-bladed putty knife*

6. *Slice off excess putty from both sides of the pane with the putty knife; leave it to harden*

Patching timber frames and sills

Faults in frames and sills
You may expect timber door and window frames to be immune from damage and deterioration – they feature no moving parts to wear out – but the action of a frequently opened (or slammed) door or casement strains hinges and can cause splits and gnarled timber. Attacks by insects and rot can also mean running repairs are called for.

If rot or insects have made a meal of the frame, the easiest option is to cut off the offending timber and let in a new section (unless severe, in which case complete replacement is best). Sagging of the frame, causing distortion and admitting draughts, can often be cured by patching or trimming the door or casement to fit the shape of the opening. In serious cases, refit the frame.

Rattling, usually caused by a warped door or casement, can be cured by reshaping the door stop, against which it closes: a planted, or separate, stop can be prised off and planed accordingly; a rebated stop, part of the outer frame, must be packed out to fill gaps.

1. Use a jigsaw (or tenon saw) to cut a wedge out of the sill around the damaged area

2. A jigsaw will cut round the back; if you don't have one, chisel it out bit by bit

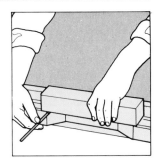
3. Cut a piece of wood roughly to fit, place it over the cut out and scribe the angled sides

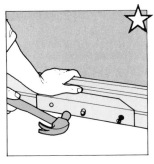
4. Glue and screw the new, preserved wood in place; fit dowels to hide the screw heads

5. Plane the infill of timber to match the surrounding sill, then prime and paint the patch

6. Carry out similar repairs to door frames where rot has damaged the timber

Repairing casement windows

Curing sticking windows
Timber windows are susceptible to sticking in their frames, through several causes. A common fault occurs when the wood swells because of moisture penetration (say if the frame is in an exposed site or the paint finish has failed). In winter, dampness in the air can have the same effect. The solution here is to plane down the edge that sticks.

Overpainting of the edges of an opening sash will also cause sticking, but removal of the finish and repainting will cure it.

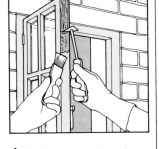
1. Apply chemical paint stripper to a heavily overpainted edge and scrape back to bare timber

Strengthening a joint
A loose joint in an opening sash will cause the window to stick in the outer frame. The problem may have been caused by shrinkage in the mortise and tenon joint, causing the sash to sag. Although the only lasting cure is to remove the frame and restick the joints, a temporary repair can be made by strengthening the joint with a metal repair bracket. With the window closed, drive wooden wedges between it and the outer frame to hold it squarely, then screw a bracket across the joint.

Curing a warped frame
A casement sash may warp out of true, with the end result that it doesn't close against the rebate. It's likely that the glass will have cracked due to the warping, and reglazing will be necessary after a repair is made.

To flatten the warped frame, lay it on a flat, firm surface and place battens on top. Use G-cramps to pull the frame flat again, so opening up the joints on the frame face. Fill the open joints with timber wedges, glued into place and planed flush.

2. Plane a few shavings from a swollen frame, taking care to keep a straight, flat edge

3. Sand the stripped or planed edge then apply primer, undercoat and top coats

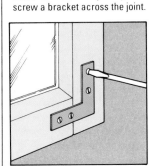
A flat metal repair bracket can be screwed across a loose joint to temporarily hold square

Pull the warped frame flat with G-cramps and drive glued wedges into the opened-up joints

Repairing Sash Windows

Cording problems

Sash, or double-hung windows – popular period features of many houses – can be the source of draughts and rattles and they're prone to mechanical defects which render them inoperative.

A sash window comprises two sashes, each sliding vertically in its own channel within an outer frame. The channels are made from three sets of beading (from inside): the staff, parting and outer. The latter may be part of the frame; the other two are separate, secured only with nails for easy removal for repairs and maintenance; the staff bead is mitred at the corners. The top sash is always the outer one. When closed, the bottom rail of the top sash is level with the top rail of the lower sash: the two parts of the window are secured with a simple catch.

So that the sashes remain at a chosen level, pairs of counter-balancing weights are attached to them by tough cords (guided by pulleys) and are housed in boxes in the sides of the outer frame. The commonest problem occurs when one or more of the cords, brittle with age or from being painted, snap, disabling the sashes. Fitting new cords – special waxed or unwaxed sets are sold to cope with a complete window – is a matter of disassembling the window, a process which usually results in the need to retouch the paintwork afterwards.

Curing rattling and jamming

Another typical fault is incessant rattling of the sashes in the wind, or even when a room door is opened or shut, due to the removable beads being too far apart. This can happen with constant use or as a result of inefficient previous repairs.

On the other hand, if the beads are fitted too tightly, are too heavily overpainted, or are set out of vertical, the sashes will be stiff, if not impossible, to slide. In either cases, repositioning and realignment of one or more of the beads is the simplest cure.

When refixing or renewing beads, it's a good idea to drill small pilot holes for the fixing nails – oval nails are best – to lessen the chance of splitting.

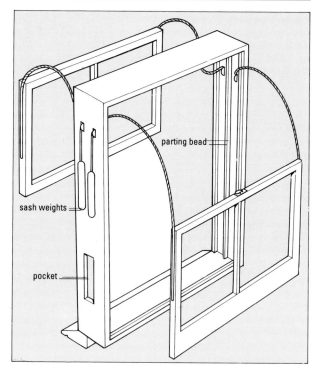

parting bead

sash weights

pocket

1. A typical sash window format, showing how inner and outer sashes are retained and slide in channels. Cords holding the sashes pass over pulleys and tie onto counter-balancing weights

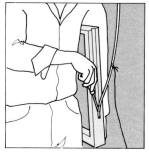

2. To free the inner sash, prise off the staff bead with a chisel near the fixing nails

3. Lift out the sash, tie string to the cord then lever the nails from their grooves

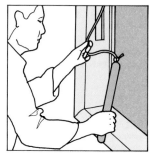

4. Lever out the parting bead – it slots in a groove – then remove the outer sash frame

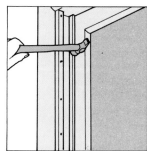

5. Lever off the pocket covers and pull out the weights and string attached to the cords

6. Free old cord, tie a new length to the string and pull over pulley and out of pocket

7. Tie on weight, hold in box above base; cut the cord to the groove length on the sash

8. Lift the sash frame into place and secure the cord in its groove with clout nails

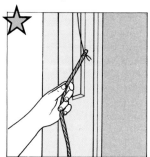

9. Replace or renew the beads with nails only, checking that they're accurately aligned

Maintaining gutters

Curing leaks and blockages

Exposed as they are, gutters can soon become clogged with leaves, birds' nests and other debris which can cause overflowing onto the house walls.

The joints between sections of guttering are their weak link; with metal gutters they're sealed with putty or mastic compounds and held together with a nut and bolt. Corrosion or defective seals can cause leaks. Proprietary mastic or paint-on sealant may cure the problem in the short term, but for a lasting solution remake the joint. Metal gutters are attached to the fascia either by separate brackets or – in the case of Ogee-section guttering – screwed direct to the fascia: loose brackets and rusted fixings can cause sagging and leaks.

Plastic gutter joints are made with union clips fitted with replaceable rubber seals; some systems incorporate clip and fixing brackets with a silt bridge to stop grit ruining the seal; others feature separate brackets. Again, sagging causing overflows is a common fault requiring the remaking of the gutters.

1. Use a trowel to remove debris from the gutter, especially near the outlets

2. To free Ogee guttering, tap the fascia screws, if rusted, with screwdriver and hammer

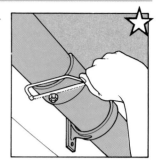

3. If you can't loosen the connecting nut and bolt, hacksaw off the nut from below

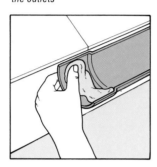

4. Free the gutter sections, scrape off the old seal then press mastic onto the joint

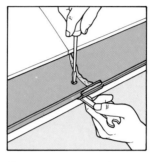

5. Fit a new nut and bolt and use a spanner and screwdriver to retighten the joint

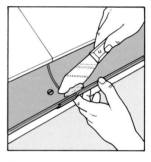

6. Use a putty knife to scrape off the mastic that's squeezed out as you tighten the nut

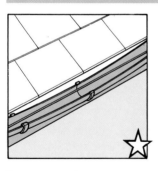

7. Check for sagging on an overflowing gutter with string stretched along its length

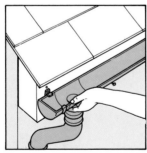

8. Cure sagging by lowering the outlet end; free it and rest on a nail in the fascia

9. Screw the gutter back onto the fascia, or reposition its clip at the new lowered level

10. Remake any joints that leak then apply bituminous paint inside a metal gutter

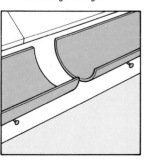

11. Support the ends of plastic guttering on temporary nails while you remake a joint

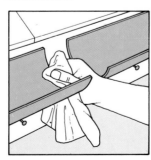

12. Clean the ends of the gutter with petrol to remove grease and perished rubber

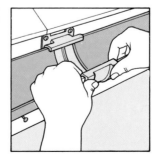

13. Remake the joint with a new rubber seal or silt bridge by snapping on the union clip

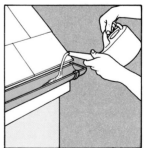

14. Finally, check that the gutter doesn't leak by pouring water in at the highest point

Maintaining downpipes

Clearing blocked downpipes

Your rainwater system is open to the elements and it's common to find that wind-blown leaves, birds' nests and other debris collect in the gutters and is washed into the downpipes. This can cause the pipes to become clogged unless you regularly clear them out.

Although you may be able to clear an obstruction from either the top or the bottom of the downpipe – say from an open hopper head or the shoe above the gully – you shouldn't allow the debris to be washed into the gully, where it could cause a blockage in the drains underground. Therefore, it's a good idea to place a suitable container over the gully to catch material as it is washed down.

Many blockages can be rodded from above using a long cane or broomhandle fitted with a padded end, although to clear an offset bend such as a swansneck at an overhanging eaves, a flexible wire or hired drain auger is a better implement to use.

Once the blockage is freed you should hose out the downpipe.

1. *Use a rubber gloved hand to pull leaves and other debris from a hopper head at first floor level*

3. *A flexible drain auger is best for clearing a blocked swansneck length of downpipe at the eaves*

2. *Rod a downpipe from the gutter outlet using a long cane or a broomhandle with a wad ram*

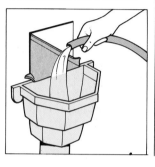

4. *When the obstruction has been cleared and removed, rinse out the downpipe with a hose*

Using an aerosol leak seal

Metal downpipes are prone to rusting, and leaks can occur in time. Although you'd be wisest to replace the entire metal set-up with a maintenance-free plastic installation, you may want to undertake a temporary repair to prevent damp walls.

A handy material to have available is a sprayable asphalt mastic, which comes in an aerosol canister. The mastic is squirted from the clog-free nozzle to form a durable, flexible coating to seal a leak – even on wet surfaces.

Squirt the asphalt mastic onto the metal downpipe in the area of the leak to form a durable seal

Securing a loose downpipe

Downpipes are secured to the house wall by brackets: on metal systems the brackets – usually part of a length of downpipe – are nailed to wooden plugs driven into the wall. On plastic set-ups the separate brackets are usually screwed into wallplugs and sometimes they are clipped to wall brackets.

Should brackets become loose, strain will be placed on the downpipe joints and there's a risk that fractures will occur.

Downpipes are always fitted from the top down so, with a metal or plastic system, refitting the brackets may call for removing the lower sections of downpipes first in order to allow higher brackets to be released.

Joints in plastic downpipes are usually made using push-fit connections with built-in rubber O-ring seals. These may be separate fittings, or as part of a length of downpipe. Faulty rings can be replaced easily.

Joints in metal downpipes are made with mastic or putty seals; clean these out and renew when the pipes are reassembled.

1. *With metal downpipes, lever the round-headed pipe nails with a claw hammer over a block*

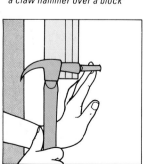

4. *The wooden plugs may have rotted: if this the case, make and hammer in new ones*

2. *If the metal pipe joint is stubborn to separate, melt the old sealant with a blowtorch first*

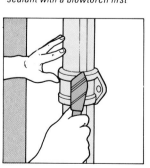

5. *Refit the section of downpipe, having pressed mastic into the socket; scrape off excess sealant*

3. *Pull the lower section of the downpipe away – the bracket is attached to a metal length*

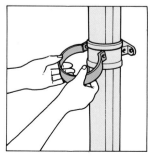

6. *With a plastic downpipe refit the wall bracket into new plugs and clip the pipe's bracket on*

Clearing waste blockages

Where waste blockages occur

If a bath, basin, sink, shower or other sanitary fitting fails to drain efficiently, it's usually because the trap underneath is blocked. In basins and kitchen sinks, soap, food-stuffs and fat are often responsible; in other fittings loose hairs may be the culprits.

In many cases you simply plunge the waste outlet using a conventional rubber plunger to release the blockage, or else use one of the many proprietary chemical remedies available. Most of these are based on caustic soda which can dissolve organic matter.

Failing these methods, you may be forced to clear the obstruction by unscrewing part or all of the trap or poking a stiff wire or special rod into the clearing eye, if one is incorporated in the trap.

With the latter methods of clearing blockages you'll have to place a bucket or bowl under the disconnected trap or waste outlet in order to catch the water in the bowl when the blockage is cleared. Alternatively, you must bail out the bowl first.

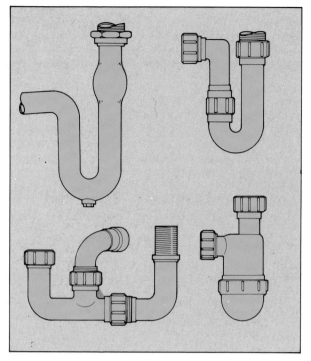

1. *Old lead traps may have a rodding eye in the base, into which stiff wire can be poked; modern plastic traps can be partially or fully unscrewed to clear the blockage*

2. *Cover the overflow with a cloth then push the plunger down sharply several times*

3. *Fish out an accumulation of hair and scum from just below the outlet with a wire hook*

4. *Use batten to counteract turning force when opening eye of a lead trap with a wrench*

5. *Hook out debris from the lead trap by poking a piece of wire coathanger through eye*

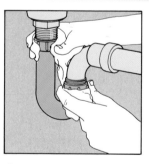

6. *A plastic U-trap can be released from the waste outlet by unscrewing the locknut*

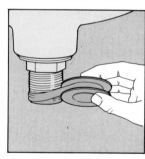

7. *If the thread of the outlet is pitted, overlap PTFE tape on the end to improve the seal*

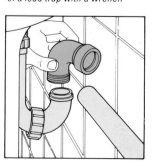

8. *In a cramped space it may be easier to release the next push-fit elbow for access*

9. *Wash out the dismantled parts of the trap to remove the blockage and any scum*

10. *With a bottle trap, grasp the waste flange connection and unscrew the base by hand*

11. *Empty the trap base then clear out residual debris before replacing the base*

Clearing gully/drain blockages

How blockages occur

Blockages in your underground drainage pipes can occur for several reasons. In gullies, the tops of which are open (although usually covered with a removable grid), leaves, twigs and other debris can be washed into the trap where they collect and form a solid barrier.

The branch drains running from soil stacks and individual sanitary fittings can become blocked by solid waste matter – such as foodstuffs, grease, paper or other materials. These drains can be cleared using hired drain clearing rods.

Clearing a blocked yard gully

Where downpipes and waste pipes discharge into a gully, a blockage in the trap – or the branch drain pipe beyond it – is identifiable by flooding.

Clearing the blockage may be a simple matter of removing leaves from the grid, or using a trowel to scoop debris from the gully trap itself. Where the obstruction has passed beyond the trap, then you will need to use drain rods to clear it.

1. *Wind-blown leaves, paper and other debris may be clogging the gully grid; remove this and clean*

2. *If the debris has passed into the gully, use a garden trowel to scoop it out of the trap*

3. *When water flows away, scrub sides with detergent to remove stubborn grease deposits*

4. *Use a garden hose to rinse out the gully and trap thoroughly. Clean the grid and replace*

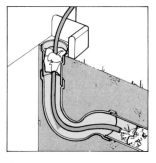

5. *Where obstruction is beyond trap feed in hose and block gully: shift debris with water pressure*

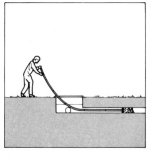

6. *Use drain clearing rods to shift or breakup a blockage via an inspection chamber*

Unblocking a drainpipe

Identify where a blockage lies by lifting manhole covers. If the gully is flooded check the nearest manhole: if it's empty, the blockage is between it and the gully; if it's flooded, check the next and if this is empty, the blockage is between it and the previous chamber. Similarly check subsequent chambers.

An interceptor trap (the last before the sewer) has a stoppered clearing eye. Remove this to drain a flooded chamber and clear the trap below with rods.

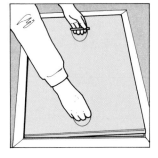

1. *Grip the handles of the manhole cover and lift with back straight and knees bent*

2. *Hired drain clearing rods have interchangeable screw, brush and plunger heads*

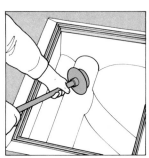

3. *Try the plunger first. Push the first rod into the 'uphill' outlet of the blocked branch pipe*

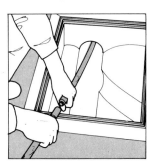

4. *Screw more rods together and feed into the pipe until you reach the blockage; plunge to shift it*

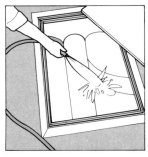

5. *When blockage is freed, scrub pipe using brush head then flush out chamber with a garden hose*

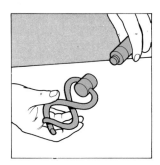

6. *If the blockage won't shift, retrieve the rods and fit a screw head; try to break up blockage*

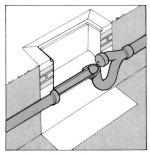

7. *Clear interceptor trap with rods or, if blockage is beyond, rod through stoppered clearing eye*

Curing tap leaks

Renewing a pillar tap washer

A tap is a valve for controlling water flow. Turn the handle anti-clockwise to raise a jumper from a valve seating in the waterway, allowing water to flow; turn it clockwise to lower the jumper and stem the flow.

A synthetic rubber washer fixed to the base of the jumper gives a watertight seal – it's this that wears with use, identified by a dripping spout. Inverting the washer may stop the drip but it's only a temporary measure and (as washers are so cheap) replacement is best.

Pillar taps are commonly used in the kitchen and comprise a capstan-handled spindle protruding from a domed easy-clean cover concealing headgear and jumper unit. The inlet rises vertically – a bib tap is similar but with a horizontal inlet.

To change the washer, isolate the supply of water to the tap and then dismantle the tap's body. Turn the water off at the mains or by closing any stopvalves (they may be under the sink), then turn on the taps to drain them completely of water.

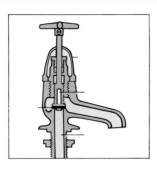

1. *The anatomy of a pillar tap showing how the jumper and washer seals the waterway*

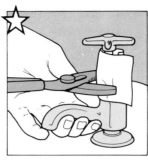

2. *Isolate tap and open valve then unscrew easy-clean cover with padded wrench if stiff*

3. *Raise easy-clean cover and insert an adjustable wrench; undo headgear nut and lift out*

4. *If the cover won't rise enough, remove handle first by releasing its side grub screw*

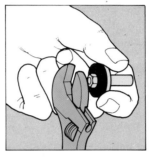

5. *Remove the headgear, pull out the jumper and undo the washer-retaining nut*

6. *Fit the replacement washer – 12mm (½in) for basins and sinks – then reassemble tap*

Rewashering a shrouded-head tap

A shrouded-head tap works in the same way as a pillar tap, although the spindle is enclosed by a metal or plastic easy-clean cover which doubles as a handle.

To remove the handle you may have to prise off the plastic 'hot' or 'cold' indicator to gain access to a cross-head screw, release a tiny grub screw in the handle or simply pull off the cover.

With the supply isolated and the tap open, rewashering is the same as for a pillar tap.

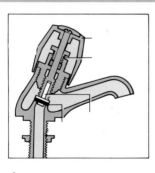

1. *The anatomy of a shrouded-head tap showing how the handle conceals the headgear*

2. *Unscrew or pull off cover, or lever off indicator cap to gain access to retaining screw*

Fitting a jumper and washer set

Sometimes with pillar and shrouded-head taps, the jumper is pegged into the headgear and can't be withdrawn, revolving in its socket. Releasing the washer-retaining nut can be a problem, unless you can grip the jumper in a vice or pliers.

It's simpler to break the pegging by pushing a screwdriver between headgear and jumper plate and to fit an all-in-one jumper and washer set: roughen the stem with a file so it grips.

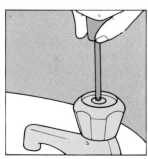

3. *Release retaining screw (you may need a cross-head screwdriver) and lift off head*

4. *Grip the spout and undo the headgear nut with an adjustable wrench and lift out*

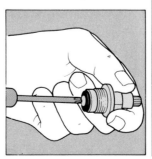

5. *Remove the faulty washer, fit the replacement then reassemble the tap body*

If you can't undo a washer-retaining nut, fit a combined washer and jumper set instead

Lifting and fixing floorboards

Lifting square-edged boards

When you need to lift floorboards for access to cables or pipes, first find out whether the boards are square-edged or tongued-and-grooved. Slot a kitchen knife between the boards to check.

The boards are usually secured to the joists with nails or brads. So long as one end of the board you wish to lift is free, you should have no trouble raising it with only a claw hammer and a bolster chisel.

Once you've lifted one board, the others should follow easily.

1. Tap in the bolster near the end of the board, holding the handle angled away from the board

Lifting a section of board

If you need to gain access to a particular part of a pipe, or an electrical accessory, there's no need to lift an entire board; you need to lift just a section.

This means cutting the board across its width but does make a handy access panel for future repairs: refix the panel on a sturdy support.

You can cut the board using a padsaw, (drill a hole with a 3mm (⅛in) diameter twist bit to start off the cut), and a tenon saw or flooring saw.

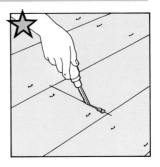

1. Drill holes for the blade against the nearest joist, then saw across at an angle

2. Prise up the board, insert the hammer claw, then slide the chisel along beneath the board

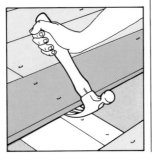

3. Lift the board, then lever up any others using the claw hammer over the joists

2. Lever up the cut end of the board about 100mm (4in) using a bolster chisel and claw hammer

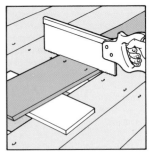

3. Wedge up the board with an offcut of wood. Saw across the board halfway over a joist

Re-fixing floorboards

If you've had to lift floorboards for any reason, it's important that you re-fix them firmly again; loose boards not only cause irritating creaks but will also form ridges under carpets or other floorcoverings.

When you prised up the boards you may have noticed that some of the fixing nails and brads remained stuck in the joists: prise these out first using a claw hammer and straighten them. Replace any really bent nails.

On old or frequently-lifted boards the nail holes often become too wide: when you re-fix the boards, position the nails to one side of the old holes, and fill the latter with filler if the boards are to be on show. Take care in this case not to damage cables or pipework nearby.

If you have to replace the board with a new one because the original split when you lifted it, you may find that the new board is somewhat thinner than its neighbours; remedy this by nailing hardboard packing pieces to the joists before you fix the new board.

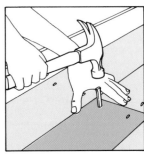

1. Invert the floorboard and tap the nails or brads back through ready for re-fixing.

2. Lower the board into the gap you've created and butt up the end to its neighbour

3. Tap the nails back in firmly but squarely and replace any that don't grip securely

4. To support a cut board end, cut a softwood batten that's just longer than a board width

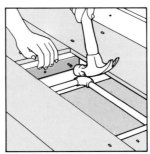

5. Skew-nail the batten to the side of the joist, butted up under the boards on each side

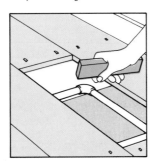

6. Drill clearance holes in the board, position it in the gap and screw it to bearer and joist

Identifying the cause of damp

Signs of dampness

Dampness is identifiable by wet, mouldy patches on walls and floors, rotten timberwork in suspended floors and roofing, and decorations, furnishings and other fixtures spoiled by mildew. It can create a humid atmosphere which is bad for health. There are two types of damp, each with symptoms whose causes may not be obvious to the untrained eye.

Causes of dampness

Penetrating damp is caused by rain infiltrating the fabric of the house. It's admitted through defective or poor quality masonry (solid walls), failed roofing, leaky rainwater gutters, cracked or torn flashings (say where a chimney emerges through the roof) and occurs in cavity walls when the ties linking the leaves are clogged with debris.

Elevations facing prevailing winds are worst affected; the dampness should normally disappear during dry spells.

Causes of rising damp

Rising damp occurs in walls and floors due to a house absorbing

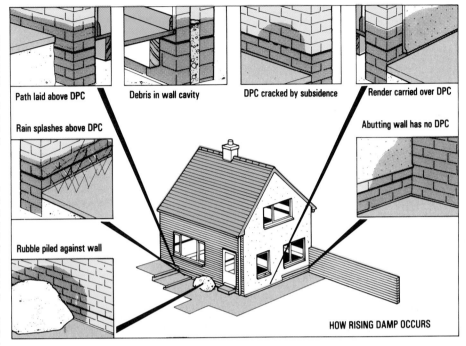

Path laid above DPC

Debris in wall cavity

DPC cracked by subsidence

Render carried over DPC

Rain splashes above DPC

Abutting wall has no DPC

Rubble piled against wall

HOW RISING DAMP OCCURS

moisture from the ground. An older house may have been built with no damp-proof course (DPC) or waterproof floor membrane

(DPM) so is vulnerable, although a newer building with DPC may be affected if the barrier breaks down, or is somehow bridged.

The problem is generally a permanent feature, becoming worse in winter when the soil's moisture content is higher.

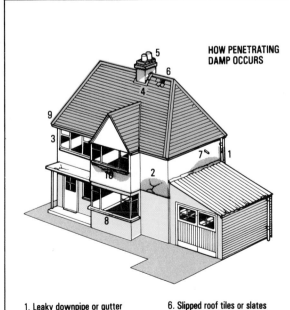

HOW PENETRATING DAMP OCCURS

1. Leaky downpipe or gutter
2. Cracked, crumbly mortar fillet
3. Defective window putty
4. Torn chimney flashing
5. Cracked chimney flaunching
6. Slipped roof tiles or slates
7. Dripping overflow
8. Blocked drip grooves
9. Damaged roof felt
10. Gaps round window frames

Testing for dampness

The presence of damp in your house might not be obvious, as some materials don't feel or look damp until they're affected quite seriously: wood doesn't feel damp until its moisture content is over 30 per cent but rot can develop at 20 per cent.

A moisture meter enables you to see how badly a material is affected: electrode pins pushed into the material gives a LED light reading against a percentage range for wood and a colour bar for various other materials.

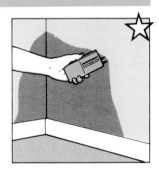

1. Trace the extent of damp using a moisture meter: a 'safe' to 'dangerous' range is used

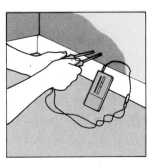

2. Deep wall probes fitted to the meter determine whether the masonry is damp within

3. Damp and condensation can be confused: a device sensitive to the latter decides

Curing rising damp in walls

Preparing inside walls

Dampness in walls won't rise more than about 1.2m (4ft), but its effects may be more pronounced in corners. If dampness is extensive, hack off the plaster 150mm (6in) above the tide mark.

Remove skirtings and check for rot in floorboards and joists. Remove radiators using lock-shield valves and release the couplings. Unclip pipe runs but leave propped in place. Turn off the electrical supply, disconnect any faceplates and fit the cores into separate connector blocks.

1. *Close radiator valves, unscrew couplers then lift radiator off brackets and drain into a bowl*

2. *With power off, remove accessory faceplates; insulate cable cores and pull back*

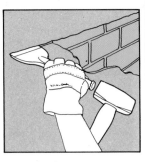

3. *Hack off all plaster just above the tide mark, taking care to avoid buried electric cables*

Injecting a chemical DPC

There are numerous types of damp proof course (DPC) that you could install, but the easiest, quickest and least disruptive method is to inject silicone-based water repellent into holes drilled in the brickwork. This lines the pores of the masonry, preventing the passage of moisture but allowing the bricks to breathe.

A chemical DPC can be injected in solid or cavity walls (if the latter are filled with insulant, check that the repellent won't react against the infill).

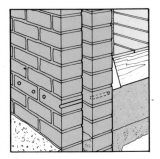

1. *With a cavity wall, drill into outer leaf, inject, drill into inner leaf and repeat*

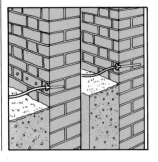

2. *In solid walls, drill two holes per stretcher, one per header; inject, drill deeper, inject again*

3. *Drill 150mm (6in) above ground, same distance below timber floor*

Using pressure-injection equipment

High-pressure injection equipment is available from hire shops, along with the water repellent fluid. Although there may be slight differences between models, most comprise an electric pump to which is attached a set of three, six or more metal nozzles.

Injectors typically have short 75mm (3in) nozzles for drilling into the single leaf of a cavity wall or from both sides of a solid wall. Longer 190mm (7½in) nozzles are used for drilling from one side of a solid wall.

Fluid is sold in 25 litre (6 gal) drums. The amount you need depends on the porosity of the masonry but allow roughly 3 litres of fluid per metre of wall.

The injector forces the fluid into the wall at a pressure of about 65 bar (95lb per sq in). With the machine on and the hose valves opened, adjust the control valve to this figure. When the surface of the bricks becomes saturated, close the hose valves and move the nozzles to the next free injection holes.

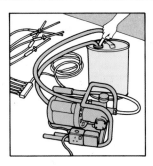

1. *Connect hoses to the injection equipment and push the feed hose well into the drum of fluid*

2. *Push the short injection nozzles into the holes and tighten the wing nuts to secure them*

3. *With some nozzles, you fit the hoses when they're inserted, using a push-fit connection*

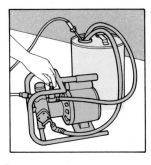

4. *Prime pump if necessary then bleed air from system through a single opened nozzle valve*

5. *Open the control valves so the fluid will be injected at the correct pressure into the wall*

6. *When bricks are saturated, move on; if injecting deeper, drill holes for long nozzles*

Curing rising damp in floors

Applying a waterproof coating

A floor that's clean, sound but showing signs of rising dampness – it may have an inadequate damp-proof membrane, or none at all – can be treated with an application of one-part moisture-curing polyurethane.

The surface must be free of grease, oil or paint films, which will all prevent absorption of the polyurethane. Repair mortar should be used for minor cracks.

Use a soft-bristled broom or large paintbrush to apply the substance. Allow about 1 litre per 5sq m (2 pints per 6 sq yards) of floor, taking the coating up the walls to join the damp-proof course (DPC).

Apply subsequent coats – four should be sufficient – at intervals of 2-3 hours when the previous finish has become tack-free. Don't delay applying the next coat or poor inter-coat adhesion will result. Apply each coat at right angles to the previous one, for complete coverage.

Three days after treatment, you can lay carpet, vinyl or other floorcoverings as required.

1. *Apply the one-part moisture-curing polyurethane to a damp floor using an old broom*

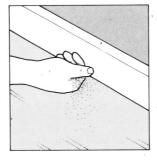

2. *Carry the polyurethane coating up the walls to connect with the house damp proof course*

3. *After about two hours, check that the polyurethane coating is tack-free before recoating.*

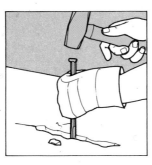

4. *Brush on subsequent coats at right angles to the previous coat for overall coverage*

5. *Sprinkle a thin layer of sharp sand over tacky final coat so it won't stick when walked on*

6. *After three days you can lay carpet or other floorcoverings on the treated surface*

Curing isolated damp spots

If a concrete floor shows only minor isolated signs of dampness emanating from cracks, the reason could be that the damp-proof membrane below the top screed has been fractured – by settlement in the foundations, for example – allowing moisture to pass through.

To make good, widen the crack, undercut its edges and clean them thoroughly. Prime the area with one-part moisture-curing polyurethane – which can be applied even to damp surfaces – to seal out the dampness. Next, fill the crack with repair mortar comprising 1 part cement: 6 parts dry sand with enough polyurethane added to make a stiff, workable paste. You shouldn't mix more of this paste than you can easily use within 20 minutes or the mortar will become too stiff to work.

Trowel the paste into the defect but don't use if the thickness will be greater than 10mm (⅜in). If cracks are larger, suspect overall failure of the floor and consider re-laying the entire slab with a new DPM in it.

1. *Widen the crack with a club hammer and chisel; undercut the edges so the mortar will grip*

2. *Remove dust and particles from the crack using a stiff-bristled banister brush*

3. *Apply a coat of moisture-curing polyurethane to seal the crack and prime the surface*

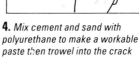

4. *Mix cement and sand with polyurethane to make a workable paste then trowel into the crack*

A hot air gun can be used to force-dry excessively damp areas of the concrete floor

Drying out the surface

Although one-part moisture-curing polyurethane can be applied to damp surfaces, ideally the concrete floor should be as dry as possible.

You can use electric fan heaters to force-dry areas plagued by excessive dampness – a hot air gun is an effective tool to use in this instance. Be sure to remove any heating equipment from the room before applying the polyurethane and never attempt to use the heater to force-dry the substance.

Curing penetrating damp

Repairing outer defences

Penetrating damp occurs when rainwater infiltrates the shell of the house. Damaged or poor quality masonry is a likely entry point. Identify the causes (see page 85) then carry out the cures. This is likely to involve repointing, rendering and sealing the brickwork and clearing clogged ties.

The roof is another prime source of trouble if tiles are cracked, broken or missing and the roofing felt beneath has been torn. The flashing seal may also require replacing.

1. *Hack back cracked or blown rendering to sound edges then spread on fresh mortar*

2. *Rake out defective mortar pointing and press in new mix then impress pointing profile*

3. *Porous masonry should be treated with coat of colourless silicone water repellent*

4. *Where damp patch is isolated on cavity wall, expose tie to remove clogging causing bridge*

5. *Where the chimney emerges from the roof, or at a lean-to roof, replace defective flashing*

6. *Torn roofing felt and missing tiles will admit rain. Fit felt patch; renew battens; retile*

7. *Seal any cracks in mortar flaunching in which chimney pots sit with flexible mastic*

Sealing windows and doors

Windows and doors are another means of entry for penetrating rain. Examine the putty sealing the glass panes: if it's crumbly, chop it out and renew it. Repair all damp, rotten timber.

Rainwater can also penetrate the house where the timber or metal frames of doors and windows adjoin the walls: seal these with mastic.

If the drip groove under a windowsill or door threshold is clogged, rain can trickle under the sill and soak the wall inside.

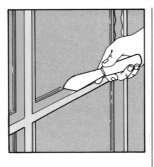

1. *Chop out defective putty, clean and prime the rebate, then press in new putty and bevel*

Guttering and plumbing leaks

Also responsible for dampness penetrating the walls of the house are faults with the rainwater collection system – the gutters and downpipes. Cast iron systems that have been in place for some time are notorious for leaking due to corrosion and are best replaced with plastic.

Plumbing problems – such as a faulty ballvalve in the cold water cistern – can manifest themselves as a constantly dripping overflow, which soaks and penetrates a wall.

1. *Clear debris such as birds' nests and leaves out of blocked, overflowing gutters and hoppers*

2. *Seal the gap between window and door frames and the sides of the opening with flexible mastic*

3. *Rake out clogged drip grooves under sills and door thresholds to stop rain trickling beneath*

2. *A cast iron guttering system is prone to leaks, so it's best to replace it with a plastic type*

3. *Rewashering a ballvalve will stop the tank overfilling and the overflow constantly dripping*

Draining water pipes

Draining the rising main

All houses have a rising main pipe which carries water to the top of the house. The rising main can serve cold taps either directly, or indirectly via a cold water storage cistern (usually situated in the loft). The kitchen cold tap is always supplied direct from the rising main.

You may need to isolate the rising main and the pipes it serves to carry out a repair or to extend the cold supply. What you do depends on your set-up.

Examine the main where it enters the house – this is usually under the kitchen sink. The pipe should be fitted with a stoptap; turning this off clockwise will prevent any more water from entering the house.

Above the stoptap there should be a draincock; by opening this with a spanner you'll be able to drain the rising main. First push a hose over the draincock nozzle and lead the free end to a suitable drainage point below the level of the stoptap.

If there's no draincock, turn on the kitchen tap to drain most of the pipe.

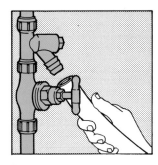

1. *Push a length of hosepipe over the nozzle of the draincock on the rising main*

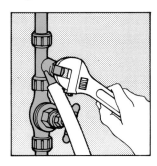

2. *Use an adjustable spanner to open the draincock and drain the water from the main*

Draining branch pipes

If you want to isolate the cold water supply pipes upstairs, it's only necessary to drain the relevant pipe instead of disabling the whole cold supply.

Look at the cold water storage cistern in the loft; if the draw-off pipes in its base are fitted with gatevalves, closing one of these will enable you to drain a particular pipe without shutting off the entire supply.

If there aren't any gatevalves, it's still a relatively simple matter to drain the pipes. First cut off the water supply to the cistern by temporarily tying up the ballvalve and then drain the cistern itself via the bathroom taps. The more cold taps you open up, the quicker the water will drain from the cistern.

If, after opening up the cold taps in the bathroom, you find that the water continues to flow, you have a direct cold water supply. With a direct system all the cold water taps in the house are connected directly to the rising main (you will find just one draw-off pipe from the cistern to the hot water cylinder).

1. *If there are gatevalves on the outlets from the cold water cistern, close the relevant one*

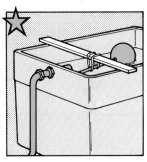

2. *Where there are no valves, tie up the ballvalve to a batten laid across the top of the cistern*

Draining hot pipes

Most homes have an indirect hot water supply system. Cold water from the storage cistern is fed to the hot cylinder, where it is heated either by an immersion heater in the cylinder or by means of a coil linked to a boiler. Hot water is taken off at the top of the cylinder to supply hot taps.

Some homes rely on instantaneous heaters for their hot water supply. These may be single-point heaters powered by gas or electricity, or else multipoint types supplying all the hot taps from one central unit and powered only by gas.

If you have an indirect system, you may be lucky enough to find gatevalves fitted on the main supply pipes at some point after they leave the storage cylinder. In this case simply turning them off will isolate the pipe run, which can then be drained by opening the appropiate hot tap. Otherwise, you have to cut off the cold supply to the cylinder at the storage cistern.

With single-point and multipoint heaters, gatevalves are fitted to isolate the cold supply.

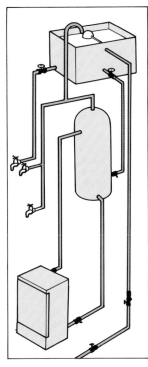

1. *On a typical indirect system you may find gatevalves and drain cocks at these locations*

2. *Cut off the cold supply to the hot cylinder by turning off the gatevalve near the cistern*

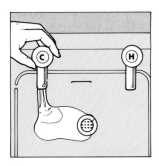

4. *Open the bathroom cold taps and run water off until the cold water cistern is empty*

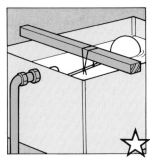

3. *If there is no gatevalve, tie up the float arm of the ballvalve or turn off the main stoptap*

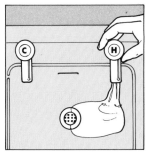

5. *Finally, turn on the hot tap on the pipe run you want to drain: some water will remain in it*

Mending burst pipes

Emergency repairs

A burst water pipe – caused by frost damage, a nail or drill inadvertently driven through, or serious corrosion, for instance – can wreak havoc, spoiling decorations and furnishings. Although turning off the supply will stop any more water entering the pipe, the immediate concern is to staunch the flow.

Space on the pipe permitting, a reusable pipe repair clamp forms an effective seal until you can isolate, drain and then repair the pipe permanently.

1. With this clamp the rubber pad is fitted over the burst and the metal plate attached

2. The two halves of the clamp connected, a wing nut is tightened to seal the hole

3. This clamp – metal plates, rubber seal and two Jubilee clips – copes with bends, too

Epoxy resin plastic putty

A repair kit that's useful to keep at hand is a two-part epoxy resin putty for use on an empty pipe.

It comes as two strips of different-coloured putty (resin and hardener), which are kneaded together then moulded round the pipe. The pipe must be rubbed with abrasive paper and cleaned with methylated spirit for the putty to bond well. Hardening takes 24 hours so the water supply will have to remain off for this time. Once hard, the repair can be sanded smooth.

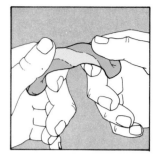

1. Tear off equal amounts of resin and hardener and knead until the colour is even

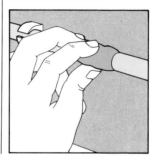

2. Clean the area of the pipe burst then mould the putty around and leave for 24 hours

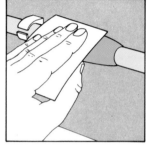

3. Once hard, the repair can be sanded smooth for neatness and the supply restored

Adhesive tape repair

Although not strictly an instant repair, as is a pipe clamp (see above), a two-part adhesive tape repair kit is an effective temporary measure, once you've drained and dried the pipe.

The first tape is wound tightly around the pipe and taken about 25mm (1in) each side of the leak. The second tape – in 150mm (6in) strips – is wound and stretched over the first and taken 25mm (1in) beyond the first. Finally more of the first tape is wound over the second.

1. Wind the first tape around the pipe, taking it 25mm (1in) each side of the burst

2. Wind second tape around pipe, each turn overlapping by half the tape's width

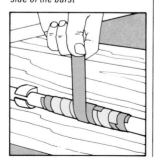

3. Finally, wind on a third layer, using the first tape, to form a waterproof seal

Replacing a burst section

One kit enables you to substitute a new length of pipe for the damaged section without soldering (or make your own kit using separately-bought parts).

The kit comprises a length of hand-bendable copper tubing and a pair of plastic push-fit connectors. To use, cut out the breached piece of pipe, push on the connectors and fit the bendable pipe between. Accuracy in cutting the pipe to length isn't important; the flexible pipe can be bent accordingly.

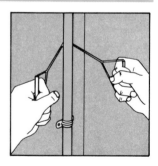

1. Drain the pipe then use a sawing wire to remove damaged piece. Prepare cut ends

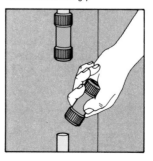

2. Slot the plastic push-fit connectors onto the lubricated cut ends of the pipe

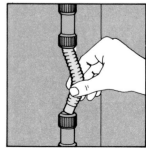

3. Push the smooth ends of the hand-bendable copper pipe into the connectors; restore supply

Tracing electrical faults

Faultfinding checklist

If something electrical fails to work around the house, you need to follow a logical procedure to isolate the problem and effect a cure. Remember to switch off the power at the fusebox or consumer unit before you investigate faults on fixed appliances or circuit wiring, and always unplug portable appliances before starting work.

Electrical appliance fails

If a portable appliance – a lamp, a kettle, or an iron, for instance – fails to work:
● Plug it into another socket – if it works, suspect a fault at the original socket
● If the appliance doesn't work, check the plug fuse and fit a new one of the correct rating
● Check the flex connections at the plug terminals and remake it; if necessary
● Remove the appliance casing and check terminal connections
● Check appliance flex continuity and replace flex if necessary
● If these checks fail, suspect a fault in the circuit, or failure of the appliance

A pendant light won't work

When a pendant light fails to work, switch off and replace the bulb. If this, too, fails:
● Switch off at the mains then check the lighting circuit fuse or MCB. Replace or reset, restore power and check light
● If the light still won't work, open the lamp's rose and check for faulty connections or broken insulation. Strip and remake, if necessary. Do exactly the same for the lampholder. Restore power and check light
● If you still have no luck or the fuse blows, disconnect flex and test continuity of cores. Replace rose and lampholder, restore power and check light. If it still won't work, suspect a fault on the whole circuit.

Circuit appears dead

If you suspect that the power or light circuit is at fault, make the following checks:
● Switch off at the mains or remove the relevant circuit fuse or trip the MCB
● Disconnect all appliances, or switch off all lights affected
● Replace the circuit fuse or reset the MCB
● Switch on the lights or plug in appliances one by one to isolate the one causing the fault
● Check, repair and replace fuse or reset MCB
● If the circuit is dead, check switches and socket outlets on the circuit for physical damage or loose connections at the terminals. Reconnect.
● Replace damaged circuit cable pierced by a drill or a nail
● If the circuit is still dead, call an electrician.

1. Test a fuse by holding it against the battery and casing of a metal torch (which should light)

2. Check plug and appliance terminal connections and remake, if necessary

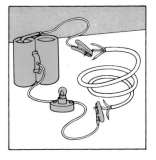

3. Test flex continuity with a torch bulb and battery, if it doesn't light, discard the flex

If the entire house system is dead

If light and power fails throughout the house, check with neighbours first; if other houses in the street are similarly troubled, the failure is a general one.

If you're the only one affected, check individual circuits, appliances and, if fitted, ELCBs. Turn all switches to off first, then replace blown fuses, remake faulty connections, and if possible, reset ELCBs. If these measures fail, call an electrician to check the main service fuse.

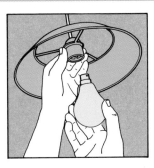

4. With a failed light, the cause may simply be that the bulb needs changing

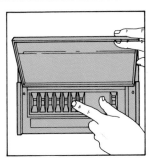

5. Before investigating circuit wiring, switch off at the mains or isolate the circuit

6. Examine the ceiling rose of a failed pendant light. Remake connections if necessary

7. Check the lampholder, too, as terminal connections may have worked loose

8. Use a lamp you know to work to check which socket outlet is faulty. Work in sequence

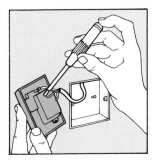

9. Use a mains tester screwdriver on a live terminal to check that the socket is dead

10. If exploration reveals a faulty fuse, repair it using the correct rating fuse wire or cartridge

Testing fuses

Causes of blown fuses

Fuses often seem to blow mysteriously, but there is always a reason that must be found before you replace them.

A fuse is a deliberate weak link, which fails in the event of any fault. Plug fuses blow if the appliance fails, while circuit fuses blow if the whole circuit is overloaded.

A short circuit in an appliance occurs when a fault allows the live current to flow straight to the neutral or earth wires, bypassing the appliance.

If all seems in order, check that the fuse is the right rating, and is not too low.

If a circuit fuse blows there may be too many appliances on it. One extra appliance is sometimes just enough to blow the fuse, even though that appliance may be perfectly sound.

The maximum rating of a ring main is 7200W; that of a radial circuit may be less.

Faulty insulation or wiring can cause either type of fuse to blow. This often happens as a result of chafing, but older wire coverings can simply rot.

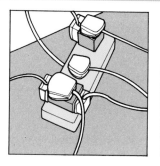

1. *Too many extension leads and adaptors can overload a single socket and cause a fuse to blow*

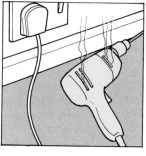

2. *If an appliance fails, a short circuit may allow a high current to flow, blowing fuse*

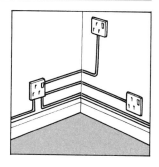

3. *Where too many spurs have been taken from one socket outlet, overloading may result*

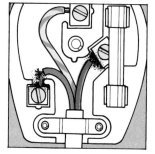

4. *Charring inside plug indicates that screw terminals of fuse have come loose*

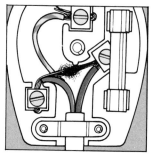

5. *Chafed wires or stray strands inside a plug can cause a short circuit and blow fuse*

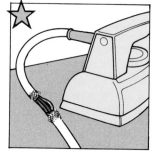

6. *Worn insulation on appliance wiring can short live and neutral wires, causing main fuse to blow*

Rewiring circuit fuses

Mending a rewirable circuit fuse

If a circuit fuse blows, first identify the reason and cure the fault (see above for the likely causes). There's no point in mending the fuse unless the cause of the blow is put right, as it would simply blow again.

With the older-type rewirable fuses, in which fuse wire is fitted between the terminals, a blow is obvious, for the wire will have melted and will be broken. Repair is just a matter of removing the old fuse wire and replacing it with wire of the correct rating.

You can buy handy cards containing lengths of circuit fuse wire of each rating, and it's a good idea to have some to hand in case of emergency. Keep it near the fuse box, along with a battery torch in case it's the lighting fuse that blows.

Before locating the faulty fuse, first switch off the power at the mains, then simply pull the fuse carriers from their sockets one at a time – unless you're certain which fuse is at fault (some installations are labelled as to which circuit a fuse serves).

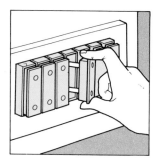

1. *With the power switched off at the mains, open the fuse box and withdraw fuses to find blown one*

2. *Use a small electrician's screwdriver to loose the screws holding the wire in the terminals*

Mending a cartridge circuit fuse

More modern electric installations use cartridge fuses, similiar to those used in appliance plugs. The cartridges simply push into grips on the terminals.

A cartridge fuse may be charred when blown, but if you're unsure test it using a battery torch with a metal casing, or a simple continuity tester

First isolate the cause of the blown fuse, cure the problem then pull out fuse and replace it with a new one.

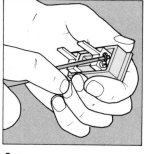

3. *Pull the broken strands of fuse wire from the carrier's terminals using the screwdriver*

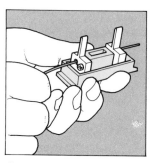

4. *Slot new fuse wire of the same rating into the carrier, wind round terminals and tighten screws*

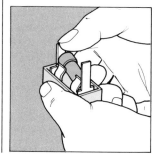

A cartridge circuit fuse can simply be pressed into the grips on the terminals in the carrier.

FABRIC STAIN REMOVAL

A

Adhesives

All types of adhesive are more difficult to remove when set; old stains should always be taken to the dry cleaners. Do not try to remove adhesives from towelling and pile fabrics, i.e. velvet. Try to work from the back of the adhesive-stained fabrics; textured weaves and fitted upholstery can be treated from fabric's right side. The following treatments are suitable for washable fabrics. **Clear household adhesive** Apply a little amyl acetate on a pad of lint-free cotton to lift out the stain. Change pad several times. **Contact adhesive** First try methylated spirit, then amyl acetate. Do not use either solvent on acetates or triacetates. **Epoxy resin** If still soft try methylated spirit; if hard take straight to dry cleaners. **Latex** Manufacturers can supply a special solvent; otherwise try a brush cleaner and restorer. **PVA wood glues** When still wet, remove excess with wet cloth, then apply neat washing-up liquid, according to fabric. **Superglue** Act immediately, saturate a cleaning pad with water and hold it on the affected area until the glue loosens. Do not attempt this treatment on napped fabric or the surface will be permanently ruined.

Alcohol

Perfume stains also come under this heading. Never delay over stain removal. **Champagne** Can oxidise on fabrics if left for even a short time. Stains turn bright yellow. Cottons, and linen unions etc., should be washed in warm sudsy water then washed at highest temperatures. **Cider/lager** On washable fabrics, mop up excess liquid with kitchen paper; sponge with sudsy water. Or soak items in cold water, then wash according to fabric, at hottest temperature. **Perfume** Soak washable fabrics immediately in warm sudsy water. Take dried-in stains on all fabrics (including washable ones) to dry cleaners. **Red wine stains** Lay white tissues under stains, if possible. Sprinkle on plenty of salt. Mix 1 tbsp borax with 1 pint warm water in plastic bucket. Soak fabric until stains disappear. Do not try diluting red wine stains by pouring white wine on

top as this can set stain even more. Take non-washable fabrics to the dry cleaners and tell them what caused the stain in the first place.

Animal stains

See Biological

B

Ballpoint

See Ink

Beer

See Alcohol: Cider/lager

Biological/animal

Protein stains (blood, milk, egg yolk, gravy etc. on washable cottons and linens (colourfast)). Soak overnight in biological detergent. Repeat if stains persist. Send woollen blankets, loose covers etc., to dry cleaners. **Excreta** On washable fabrics, scrape off any deposits with blunt knife. Rinse well under running cold water. Soak white cotton and linen in a solution of bleach – 1 eggcupful to 1 gallon of cold water – for 2-3 hours. Launder in heavy duty detergent. Non-washable fabrics: treat with pads of absorbent kitchen paper, cold water and ammonia solution: 1 part ammonia to 3 parts water. Blot excess and take straight to dry cleaners. **Urine** Blot up excess with absorbent kitchen roll. Then rinse in cold water. Soak white cottons in bleach solution (see Excreta), then launder in heavy-duty detergent. For wool and for fitted upholstery, sponge with absorbent kitchen paper and solution of vinegar: 1 cupful to 1 pint of water. Blot thoroughly with lots of absorbent kitchen paper, then take to dry cleaners, or call in an expert from a reputable cleaning firm.

Bleach

Stains by most bleaches cause immediate colour loss from non-fast dyed fabrics. Either re-dye the same colour if fabric can be dyed, or camouflage small marks on cotton and linen union prints with fabric paints.

Butter

See Grease

C

Candlewax

One of the few times heat is applied. Pick or scrape off excess with blunt knife or fingernail. Then sandwich stained area between two sheets of absorbent kitchen paper and press with a warm iron. Change paper each time wax is absorbed. Use a grease solvent on residue then wash as normal. For upholstery, place absorbent paper on fabric and press. Wipe off residue with a grease solvent then treat with a little upholstery shampoo. Sponge with clear water. Blot dry with absorbent paper.

Chewing/bubblegum plasticine/putty

Pick off any excess beforehand. Treat small amounts with solvent cleaner. Alternatively put ice cubes in a plastic bag and hold against gum to harden, then pick off. (Do not use this last method on pile fabrics; these should be taken to the dry cleaners.)

Champagne

See Alcohol

Chocolates/soft sweets

Scrape off residue with blunt knife. Dab solvent spot remover onto stain.

Cocoa

See Coffee

Cod liver oil

See Grease

Coffee/Tea/Cocoa

Non-washable fabrics should be dry cleaned. Duvets may well need special treatment from manufacturers as fillings may be affected. PVC fabric stained on non-laminated side may respond to sponging with biological powder solution and warm water if treated immediately. Cocoa dye residues can be treated with methylated spirits.

Cream

See Grease

Curry

It is the turmeric in curry that leaves

such a persistent yellow stain on table linen; it is a vegetable dye that can be very difficult to remove. For non-washable fabrics, dry cleaners suggest treating mishaps with a drop of olive oil or eucalyptus oil as this suspends dye colour. Items should then be taken in for dry cleaning. White table linen can be treated with neat washing-up liquid and then spot-treated with a proprietary dye remover. Finish by soaking the linen in a fabric brightener.

D

Dyes-fabric/henna and hair colourants

Dye colours on white, washable fabrics can be treated with a proprietary dye remover, but do not use on non-colour fast fabrics. Henna and other hair colourants can leave stains on household furnishings. These usually wash out if treated to overnight soaking in detergent; heavier stains may need bleaching: 1 eggcupful bleach to 1 gallon water. Wash in heavy-duty detergent. Henna acts as a bleach on non-fast deep dyed articles; see **Bleach** for suggested remedies. For henna stains on white woollen fabrics use hydrogen peroxide in a 20 vol solution (ask in your local chemist for the correct solution): 1 part to 4 parts water.

E

Eggs
See Biological

F

Felt-tip pens
See Ink

Fruit/vegetables

Worst culprits are fruit squash and lollipop stains on non-washable fabrics. These can disappear into light coloured loose covers only to reappear after dry cleaning as untreatable 'caramelized' brown stains. For washable fabrics, soak overnight in a branded product of fabric brightener. Work washing-up

liquid or detergent into the remaining residues and wash according to fabric.

Furniture polish

Misfiring with aerosol sprays can cause mishaps to upholstery and curtains. Work in neat washing-up liquid and wash out. For thicker, greasy polishes, scrape off excess with a knife, then treat with washing-up liquid, wash out, blotting up excess moisture with absorbent kitchen paper. Non-washable fabrics should be dry cleaned.

G

Glue
See Adhesives

Grass

Try a saturated pad of methylated spirits on the wrong side of the fabric, pushing out stain the way it came in. Small grass stains on white fitted upholstery and furnishing fabrics may respond to a branded product paste cleaner.

Gravy
See Biological

Grease/oils/shoe polish

Treat heavy stains on washable fabrics with a solvent-based cleaner containing carbon tetrachloride, then wash at the hottest temperature fabric can take. For upholstery, a paste dry cleaner can be used for grease stains on white fabrics; heavily ingrained areas and pile fabrics may need professional cleaning.

H

Hair lacquer

Treat fabric first with a cotton pad soaked in acetone or amyl acetate.

Honey
See Jam

I

Ink

You must identify the type of ink before you do anything else at all, since the

wrong treatment can set stains irretrievably. Small recent stains can sometimes be treated on washable fabrics, but all others, including old ink stains, should be taken to the dry cleaners. **Ballpoint** Saturate pad with methylated spirit or proprietary brand of ballpoint pen remover. Wash in warm sudsy water. Take stubborn stains and those on washable fabrics to the dry cleaners. **Felt-tip** Water-soluble stains can be held under cold running water until most of the colour has gone, then wash as usual. Others respond to blotting and pressure with a pad of methylated spirits or branded removal product. Treat residues with liquid detergent, working this well into fabric. **Permanent ink** Seek professional advice. **Washable ink** Recent stains on washable cottons can sometimes be sponged out with cold water before washing in heavy duty detergent. Small brown marks that remain, can then be treated in the same way as rust and iron mould stains.

Iron mould
See Rust

J

Jam/marmalade/ honey/syrup

For washable fabrics, scrape off excess with blunt knife, then blot with absorbent kitchen paper. Apply neat washing-up liquid or liquid detergent, massaging well into fabric. Rinse out in cold water and launder according to fabric. Non-washable fabrics must be dry cleaned as soon as possible.

L

Lipstick
See Make-up

M

Make-up/mascara foundation/lipstick

On washable fabrics, remove surplus with blunt knife. Treat with solvent cleaner. Massage any residues with liquid detergent or washing-up liquid. Before this dries, launder thoroughly in heavy duty detergent.

Mayonnaise
On washable fabrics, scrape off excess with blunt knife then treat with neat washing-up liquid. Alternatively, soak overnight in a biological detergent (read the instructions carefully).

Metal polish
On washable fabrics, dab with pad saturated in white spirit. When dry use a soft brush to remove powdery residues. Launder in heavy-duty detergent according to fabric. For upholstery, seek professional advice.

Mildew
If recent, wash in heavy-duty detergent. Dry out in strong sunlight. Soak white cotton and linen fabrics in bleach solution – one tablespoon to 2 pints of water – then wash thoroughly. Unsightly marks usually disappear with repeated careful laundering.

Milk
See Biological

Mud
On washable fabrics, allow to dry out thoroughly before gently brushing out; treat any stubborn residues with neat washing-up liquid, then wash carefully according to fabric.

Mustard
See Jam

N

Nail polish
See Paint: Cellulose

Newsprint
See Grease

O

Oils
See Grease

Orange juice
See Fruit/vegetables

P

Paint
Unless treated instantly, most paints will need professional stain removal once they have dried hard, whether fabrics are washable or dry clean only. Never try to remove paint from pile fabrics. Different paints require stain removal treatments as follows: **Cellulose modelling paints/nail polishes** Try acetone or amyl acetate. (Do not use on acetates or triacetates.) **Emulsion (acrylic)** Try dabbing with a little methylated spirits while still wet. Take dried stains to dry cleaners. **Gloss/oil paint** If still wet, try blotting with a pad saturated with a solvent cleaner. Do not wash or the stain may set. **Polyurethane varnish** Try white spirit on wet stains, then liquid detergent as usual.

Perfume
See Alcohol

Polish
See Metal polish and Grease.

Plasticine
see Chewing gum.

Putty
See Chewing gum.

R

Rust
Stains are caused by metal fastenings; clogged-up steam irons can also spatter rust. On white washable fabrics, recent stains may respond to painting with diluted citric acid dissolved in a little water. Failing that, use a proprietary rust remover. The traditional method is to use a diluted solution of oxalic acid in a 3 per cent solution, painting this on affected areas. Oxalic acid is very toxic, however, so use it and dispose of it carefully. Wear rubber gloves when using, and mix it in a ceramic or glass bowl. Ask your pharmacist for details about mixing the solution and disposing of it safely after use. To prevent rust mould stains appearing, rinse items thoroughly after treatment in purified water (available, in bottles, from any large chemist).

S

Scorch marks
Nothing can be done about heavy scorch marks. Light ones on white wool can be treated with diluted hydrogen peroxide. Always seek expert advice about cigarette burns, since some dry cleaners can arrange for invisible mending or reweaving to be carried out.

Shoe polish
See Grease

Sun tan oil
If cleaning in situ, rub a little washing-up liquid into the stain, then wipe with a clean cloth. On removable fabric, dab eucalyptus oil around edge of stain, working inwards; place an absorbent pad under stain and press down firmly.

T

Tar
Remove excess tar with blunt knife. Tie-off stain from rest of fabric with piece of string. Dip stain into bowl containing proprietary tar remover; repeat, then wash fabric as hot as possible.

Tea
See Coffee

U

Urine
See Biological

V

Vomit
See Biological

W

Wax polish
See Grease

Wine
See Alcohol

INDEX